LIVING WITH
HEAVEN'S
GLORY MINDSET

LIVING WITH HEAVEN'S GLORY MINDSET

31 DAYS OF KINGDOM GLORY

FELIX HALPERN

© Copyright 2023– Felix Halpern

All rights reserved. This book is protected by the copyright laws of the United States of America. This book may not be copied or reprinted for commercial gain or profit. The use of short quotations or occasional page copying for personal or group study is permitted and encouraged. Permission will be granted upon request. Scripture quotations marked KJV are taken from the King James Version. Scripture quotations marked NIV are taken from the HOLY BIBLE, NEW INTERNATIONAL VERSION®, Copyright © 1973, 1978, 1984, 2011 International Bible Society. Used by permission of Zondervan. All rights reserved. Scripture quotations marked NKJV are taken from the New King James Version. Copyright © 1982 by Thomas Nelson, Inc. Used by permission. All rights reserved. Scripture quotations marked NASB are taken from the NEW AMERICAN STANDARD BIBLE®, Copyright © 1960, 1962, 1963, 1968, 1971, 1972, 1973, 1975, 1977, 1995, 2020 by The Lockman Foundation. Used by permission. Scripture quotations marked AMP are taken from the Amplified® Bible, Copyright © 2015 by The Lockman Foundation, La Habra, CA 90631. All rights reserved. Used by permission. Scripture quotations marked ESV are taken from The Holy Bible, English Standard Version® (ESV®), copyright © 2001 by Crossway, a publishing ministry of Good News Publishers. Used by permission. All rights reserved. Scripture quotations marked NLT are taken from the Holy Bible, New Living Translation, copyright 1996, 2004, 2015. Used by permission of Tyndale House Publishers, Wheaton, Illinois 60189. All rights reserved. Scripture quotations marked CEB are taken from The Common English Bible Copyright © 2010 by the Common English Bible Committee and the Christian Resources Development Corporation Inc. (CRDC), Nashville, Tennessee. All rights reserved. Used by permission. Scripture quotations marked TLB are taken from The Living Bible; Tyndale House, 1997, © 1971 by Tyndale House Publishers, Inc. Used by permission. All rights reserved. All emphasis within Scripture quotations is the author's own. Please note that Destiny Image's publishing style capitalizes certain pronouns in Scripture that refer to the Father, Son, and Holy Spirit, and may differ from some publishers' styles. Take note that the name satan and related names are not capitalized. We choose not to acknowledge him, even to the point of violating grammatical rules.

DESTINY IMAGE® PUBLISHERS, INC.
P.O. Box 310, Shippensburg, PA 17257-0310
"Promoting Inspired Lives."

This book and all other Destiny Image and Destiny Image Fiction books are available at Christian bookstores and distributors worldwide.

For more information on foreign distributors, call 717-532-3040.

Reach us on the Internet: www.destinyimage.com.

ISBN 13: 978-0-7684-7426-8

Ebook: 978-0-7684-7427-5

For Worldwide Distribution, Printed in Columbia

1 2 3 4 5 6 7 8 / 27 26 25 24 23

Contents

Preface	A Step-by-Step Guide: 31 Steps in 31 Days	1
	Getting Ready	3
	Morning Prayer for Each Day	9
	Ending Meditation for Each Day	10
Step 1 / Day 1	Invite His Greatness into Your Day	12
Step 2 / Day 2	The Day of the Psalmist	17
Step 3 / Day 3	A Day of Exploration	24
Step 4 / Day 4	Leaving the Monkey Mind	31
Step 5 / Day 5	Applying the Gospel	35
Step 6 / Day 6	Learning Scale of Importance	40
Step 7 / Day 7	Inside-Out Living	44
Step 8 / Day 8	Focus on the Potter	49
Step 9 / Day 9	Learning to Feel Again	54
Step 10 / Day 10	Exercise Faith Today	60
Step 11 / Day 11	Dare to Be Right	65
Step 12 / Day 12	Marks of a Davidic People	72
Step 13 / Day 13	Day of Compassion	79
Step 14 / Day 14	Meditate on His Power	83
Step 15 / Day 15	Day of Your Soul	89
Step 16 / Day 16	Learning the Principle of Yield	94
Step 17 / Day 17	Adoption and Sonship	101
Step 18 / Day 18	Right Perspective	107

Step 19 / Day 19	Safe-Haven Moments	113
Step 20 / Day 20	Issues of the Heart	119
Step 21 / Day 21	Sin of the Golden Calf	124
Step 22 / Day 22	Detachment	129
Step 23 / Day 23	Humility: The Great Physician	134
Step 24 / Day 24	Having a Glory Perspective	139
Step 25 / Day 25	Crowns: Which Do You Want?	144
Step 26 / Day 26	Having Self-Control	151
Step 27 / Day 27	A True Disciple	156
Step 28 / Day 28	Morning Jump Exercise	162
Step 29 / Day 29	Setting Your Spiritual Temperature	167
Step 30 / Day 30	To the Jew First	173
Step 31 / Day 31	Honoring Israel and the Jewish People	178
Bonus Day	Seek First the Kingdom	183

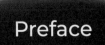

Preface

A Step-by-Step Guide: 31 Steps in 31 Days

My time recording my adventure has now been completed. We have turned convention on its head again and again, and have done enough pinpricking here to last us for a long time. We have covered the necessary dance steps for you to enter a life of dancing past the darkness, and now with some intentionality seasoned with a dose of desperation for change, you will succeed.

As *Heaven's Soul Cleanse* addressed the soul, the following devotional provides steps to take daily. The goal is to incorporate them into your life. This 31-step adventure and devotional stretches out over 31 days. Most of the themes were covered in *Dancing Past the Darkness,* and came out with me from the glory side that began in September 2019.

Once you read *Dancing Past the Darkness,* it prepares you to go on a 31-step, 31-day adventure living the glory and kingdom in your daily life. I hope each day is like a basket of fresh-out-of-the-oven spiritual delicacies, and your ears are perked enough to keep going, pressing in for more. Each day has a theme, a prayer, and an opportunity to make an entry in your journal that is provided.

My overall message is that you're never alone and that God teaches us how to handle life's challenges. Neither money nor material extras will make His children feel secure, but only His abiding presence will supply every need we have. Take these teachings as diamonds in the rough to polish, so they shine forth the Kingdom's glory in you.

Getting Ready

THE INSPIRATION FOR THIS DEVOTIONAL CAME OUT OF THE glory side, Heaven, and the sea of love that our Father has for us. In the quietly removed world of Heaven, we can only dream together and plan our future eternity, made possible by a love that knows no bounds. Earthly life, compared to Heaven, is like a thin strip of parkland—gray, with dry, withered bushes. The earth pales in comparison to God's glorious love for you. I want to stop you at the edge of your morning, to contemplate an entranceway to the presence of God. This morning is the first day, so by setting the atmosphere of your heart, we begin where it all started.

It wasn't long after I came to faith that I realized God smiled kindly upon me, when He invited me into a relationship with the one true God of Heaven. No longer a standard poor man's meal, spiritually speaking, but a feeding fit for a king began. It is still the most incredible love story ever told, and a spiritual banquet that resides within us. Can you remember when your heavenly Father sent His only Son into your heart? Do you remember the day and time when He captured your love? "Take me away with you—let us hurry! Let the king bring me into his chambers" (Song of Solomon 1:4 NIV). How we rejoice to delight in His marvelous light and enjoy praising His love more than wine. How right we are to adore Him!

Why is it that such words come when we think of our Groom?

Why is it that such thoughts overflow our souls?

Because the Holy One, blessed be He, marvelously ambushed us. There is something about Him that you know you can trust. When the Son of God descended to earth, it was without fanfare, pomp, or circumstance. He came to us as a lowly servant, yet submerged in the richness of the Father's love for us. One cannot help but notice His self-sacrifice, His life freely offered, wanting nothing in return. The glories of Heaven are left behind willingly, voluntarily, bringing us love unsparingly, only to be born into an ordinary family with no material means (see Matthew 1:1-17).

Although he was born of the line of David, through royal descent, He was the true prophesied Jewish Messiah (see Luke 1:32-33; Hebrews 1:5; Jeremiah 23:5-6; Acts 15:15-16; Psalm 2). When He arrived, He chose a simple life. He knew the sweat of the brow and made the helpless and hopeless His friends. He showered with compassion all those forsaken by society and scarred by disease. As He went from town to town, He was inclined to talk to strangers when no one would. He taught us that God had not forgotten or abandoned us to life's miseries.

He showered us with God's love despite our sins and failures, revealing to all who listened that God hears our every cry and petition. He would say, "Never mind about your problems; give them to Me, and I will carry them" (see Matthew 11:30). Our tears are washed away with hope—and someday, we will be taken home to be with Him forever (see Revelation 21:4).

But the story goes back further.

The genuine source of our life comes from God's primordial (ancient, primal, and instinctive) love. It joins us to something greater, and more important than ourselves, deeper and abiding. Once we experience His love, worldly pursuits dim. For me it was like taking a hammer to the things of the world, shattering a window, hard, fast. The glass crackles into a webbed pattern, finally sagging and falling to the ground. We are free! It's the purpose of our redeemed self.

If we were to return to the start of creation, we would find that God created man in His image. In one extraordinary time, intimate fellowship existed between the Father and Adam and Eve. A physicality between them was enjoyed, as they could hear God walking in the Garden in the cool of the day. God was present (see Genesis 3:8), and there was no need for Adam and Eve to venture out of the Garden.

When satan deceived Adam and Eve the wind of the spirit stopped.

All creation grew in a quiet breath to near-perfect silence, and this unimaginable intimacy and physicality were forfeited.

All creation felt the sting. However, that is not the end of the story; it is here that we find our way into the drama of the ages.

God then set out to establish a family of faith through whom He could restore intimacy through a chosen people. They would reveal the heavenly Father to fallen humanity, and be raised as a standard-bearer nation; Israel and the Jewish people. This nation would proclaim—through the Torah, a festal life, and the sacrificial system—the principles and precepts of God that would move the world toward the ultimate sacrifice of His Son.

Then, upon the Jewish Messiah's advent, and the Jewish prophets' fulfillment, the New Covenant body carried this mission forward. Matthew 24:14 (NIV) states, *"And this gospel of the kingdom will be preached in the whole world as a testimony to all nations, and then the end will come."* This end will be ushered in by none other than the Messiah of Israel:

> *Then cometh the end, when he shall have delivered up the kingdom to God, even the Father; when he shall have put down all rule and all authority and power. For he must reign, till he hath put all enemies under his feet. The last enemy that shall be destroyed is death. For he hath put all things under his feet. But when he saith all things are put under him, it is manifest that he is excepted, which did put all things under him* (1 Corinthians 15:24-27 KJV).

In this passage, we are presented with God's plan for the earth—one day it will be filled with God's knowledge, glory, and love. The two are inseparable. Independent of this final plan, God's Son, the first King, will return and remain the only King until the end. All other powers will be destroyed, and to Him all nations will come and give Him praise and honor (see Psalm 117:1; 1 Chronicles 29:10-13; Zechariah 3:20).

However, we can lose awareness through our busyness and earthly activities, that the world is our oyster for our individual use. God is the master architect of this oyster, the earth, and He did not create it out of a crucible of pain, as a woman in labor, or war and struggle as nations are born. Hebrews 1:10 (NIV) refurbishes our understanding of this: *"In the beginning, Lord, you laid the foundations of the earth, and the heavens are the work of your hands."*

Again, we return to the fact that we live because of His love. Yet, we are never forced to love our Father, but invited into His love chamber. Isn't this true love? Anyone who hears this story will have tears gather in their eyes because there is something lovely and life-altering when this story is told. When people hear this love story, they confess their sins. They ask for forgiveness, and they are filled with joy and assurance. Enjoy His love for you today, and look for someone to share it with. How can we ignore it?

Journal

Write your thoughts of His love when you came to faith. Carry them with you this morning, by letting your love story be the sweet wind in your sail throughout your day.

_____

_____

_____

_____

_____

_____

_____

_____

_____

Living with Heaven's Glory Mindset

Morning Prayer for Each Day

O Lord of eternity—O Lord of eternity.

Help me find You more in my life daily so I may know more of You. Help me awaken Your greater, deeper, and more profound presence and glory through Your Holy Spirit. Sanctify each living moment of this day living in communion with You.

O Lord of eternity, I call You my present help in times of trouble. You are where my heart resides. Lift me, O Lord, lift my soul to a higher and deeper state of awareness of Your blissful peace through the sacrifice of Your Son. May I enter the eternal now with You, living each day for You while in this mortal realm.

O Lord of infinity—O Lord of infinity.

Help me recognize the abundance of Your blessings in each moment as new possibilities.

Help me realize that each possibility is a manifestation of Your love.

Help me be centered in Your presence and glory today, O Lord, that I may embrace each possibility as an opportunity to serve You as a channel of blessings to others, and thus glorify You.

O Lord of eternity—here I am.

O Lord of infinity—here I am.

O Lord of majesty—here I am.

O Lord of life and salvation—here I am.

Ending meditation for each day

Lord, thank You for being with me today.

Where would I be without You, O Lord?

Where would I be without You?

Where would the earth be without You, O Lord?

Without You, we would not be.

Without Your breath, we would not have the air of Heaven to breathe.

Without Your love, we would not know love; we could not give love to others.

Without You, O Lord, tears of compassion could not run from our eyes, and empathy would not have sway over our hearts.

The world would be cold, dark, and left to the destroying one.

Without You, the morning bird would not be heard.

The lilies of the valley would not be seen.

The outstandingly dressed birds of paradise would be dark and gray.

The trees of the field could no longer clap their hands.

The heavens could not proclaim Your glory and Your majesty.

To be left alone without You is too fearful to consider.

Ending Meditation for Your Day

To be with You, words are insufficient.

You, O Lord, are our peacemaker in the evening.

You, O Lord, are the first to greet us in the morning.

You, O Lord, always remain our Sabbath peace.

You, O Lord, maker of Heaven and earth, are the Potter, crafting my life. You are the Waymaker of my days.

You are Lord, who You say You are!

You act in righteousness and justice, never provoked as a man.

Trustworthy, worthy of all hope and faith are You alone.

Lord, You show me how to love one another as we love ourselves. Only You made this possible, Lord!

Only in You is this possible.

We love ourselves because You loved us first and gave Your life for us. We love ourselves because of the dignity that You gave us as Your children.

All that we are is from You.

All that we hope is from You.

You are an ocean of love whose depths we are yet to plumb.

You are our oasis in the desert; rain in a parched land; the wind that fills our sails; the strength that sustains our bodies. You're a bright morning star in times of darkness.

Oh yes, Lord! Where would we be without You? I cannot imagine a day with You!

Step 1 / Day 1

INVITE HIS GREATNESS INTO YOUR DAY

As you wake this morning, recall that His glorious throne of justice rests over you despite the countless troubles in the world today. His foundation of old remains the source of all truth, justice, righteousness, and love. Where the foundations of the world shake and tatter, His remains unmoved.

So it is with your life.

You have learned what past generations have learned—no hope exists without Him. To this truth, you live before a cloud of many witnesses (see Hebrews 12:1). So this is your hope again as you begin your day. This hope is like a coin that you carry in your pocket throughout the day.

Every pulse of your heart rests under His dominion. Faithfulness is His steady rain for you, and as a mighty, clear running spring breaks through and rises from the ground, righteousness soaks your soul. Just lift your hands to Heaven this morning and say, "Thank You, Lord."

Ask, "Lord, rain on me this morning!"

"Yes, Lord, soak me!"

The Lord will give you what is good today, and the day will yield its increase in this time of rain. Embrace the steadfast love and faithfulness of Him as they kiss you this morning.

Remember! He is excellent. He moves in beautiful ways (see Isaiah 55:8-9). He also moves in mysterious ways; His ways are not ours (see Ecclesiastes 3:11). But amid the mystery, your life has been decreed from beginning to end when He gave you the steadfast and holy one—Yeshua, Jesus. Without Him, we would be lost in a deep forest of despair, swept away like a piece of driftwood in the ocean. You, Lord, have become my hope; only You are the utmost Holy One.

Invite His glory into your day today!

Invite Him into your situation to sit with you!

Invite His greatness into your thoughts to overshadow the world!

Invite Him to shower you with His rain, and let Heaven dictate your steps and thoughts today.

For I have been the source of all your truth, says the Lord. I am justice, righteousness, and My love for you has endured from generation to generation. Without Me, no hope exists. With Me, hope radiates through each hour of your day. Every impulse, pulse of your heart, thought, and action comes under My dominion today. Never do I leave you or forsake you. Never is cruelty or insensitivity found in Me, says the Lord. Steadfast love and faithfulness meet righteousness, and peace kisses you. So get ready!

ACTION STEP

Work at seeing God in everything around you today—in situations, conversations, and problems. Look through the busyness and situations of the day to see the faithfulness of God and His glory. Someone gives their life to the Lord every moment on God's earth, and the Kingdom enlarges. Someone is getting healed; the blind are receiving their sight; someone somewhere has become the subject of a miracle. Stay in the light and away from the shadows in your day.

Prayer

Lord, thank You for Your excellent greatness and majesty. Your comprehensible perfection is beyond compare. Nothing in this world is more fantastic and marvelous. Let me see Your glorious glory today and bask in the shadow of Your greatness.

Journal

Record your meditations and thoughts of the magnificence of God throughout your day. Offer one experience or revelation that stood out in your day.

> *If anyone thinks they are something when they are not, they deceive themselves* (Galatians 6:3 NIV).
>
> *Trust in the Lord with all your heart, and lean not on your own understanding* (Proverbs 3:5 NKJV).
>
> *Keep your heart with all vigilance, for from it flow the springs of life* (Proverbs 4:23 ESV).

Invite His Greatness into Your Day

Living with Heaven's Glory Mindset

STEP 2 / DAY 2

The Day of the Psalmist

Today you will step into the heart of the psalmist, learning to pray as the psalmist prayed. Thousands have experienced *Heaven's Soul Cleanse* to experience the lifting of their souls by spending 31 days in the glory of God. It has spawned groups called "little psalmists," whereby men and women are drawing from their meditations in the spirit and language of the psalmist. The book of Psalms is the only book in the Bible that is "the handbook of the soul," because it teaches us about our relationship with our soul. More is spoken in this book concerning the soul than in any other book in the Bible.

- The soul can be estranged from the womb (see 58:3).
- The soul waits and thirsts for God (see 62:1-2; 63:1-2).
- The soul needs to cling to God (see 63:8).
- The soul needs to hear what God has done (see 66:16).
- God draws near to the soul and gladdens the soul (see 69:18).
- He commands his soul to bless the Lord (see 103:1-5).

- The soul was created to worship the Lord in the splendor of His majesty (see Psalm 96). Proverbs 20:27 (KJV) says, *"The spirit [soul] of man is the candle of the Lord."* Harness the soul; Yeshua is glorified.

In other words, whenever you choose to make known the will of God, the soul there goeth my friend, and this candle of the Lord burns brighter. If *"The Spirit* [soul] *of man is the candle of the Lord,"* according to Proverbs 20:27, what occurs?

Today's devotion will whet your spiritual appetite. Sit still somewhere where you can only hear your breathing. Let your spirit ascend the mountain of the Lord with meditations and exaltations from within your soul. Cease from all petitions today.

Today, no petition, praise, or thanksgiving for all that He has done for you. This day is dedicated to being a "lover" of Him only. It's not about "I," "me," "mine," or "our." I want you to experience what the Lord said to me upon my return from Heaven: "Let not your silence be tainted by desires, wants, and needs, for they will only distract you from the living present, I AM. Let no vague impressions of your past and shadowy images of the future lead you astray from what I desire for you. Rather, let your silence be receptive to the light of My presence, for I am the Holy One of Israel that dissolves all tainted desires and thoughts."

You see, God desires to release affection from a hidden cavernous well in you, so that your smile will not falter, and your Father's smile will be found. With a shuddering breath, you'll be bouncing with excitement. Imagine 31 days of love where you can feel His stare. I want to show you how to settle yourself under His arms, and lean into Him again—wholly lifting Him up and showering Him with your love. You'll experience the pleasure of your Father. Here is one testimony of one of the thousands that have undertaken the 30-day soul cleanse:

> I believe this is a key to freeing people, especially at a time like this. I hear many people having mental issues and committing suicide. I experienced anxiety in the past but not to the point that I would experience pain in my back and shoulders. You showed me how to focus on God more and detach myself from my needs and worries.
>
> Not praying for my needs challenges me to trust in Him more and depend more on His sovereignty, promises, and unfailing love for me. Resting and waiting on Him humbles me, makes me more reverent for Him and allows me to think about who He is more without doing the to-do list, like praying for one hour, declaring His promises over my situation to make sure my prayers are answered.
>
> I used to do a lot of transactional prayers. Letting go of control, trusting God that His will be done, and enjoying His presence are freeing feelings. Anyway, this is just what I learned about myself in trying to do this soul cleanse. Thank you.

Let's begin here with your early morning musings. Go slowly and make the following prayer your own as the following psalms inspire you. Today your only reading should be the psalms given below.

Instructions

Do no further reading today than what is offered below. Allow them to marinate in your soul. Read slowly, and let it become your prayer and personal meditation to the Lord. Your meditations may take on the flavor of one of the "small psalmists" below.

> O Lord, You feed Your flock when our souls are devoid of morality and righteousness.
>
> Your table is always set!
>
> You, Lord, prepare a sumptuous banquet that fills us with tranquility and wisdom foreign to this world.
>
> Splendid is this divine cuisine!
>
> O Lord, You are the Bread of Life who sustains us throughout our trials and without payment.
>
> Delightful is the meal!
>
> You, Lord, and Your miraculous manna feed us in the stark wildernesses of this world.
>
> Enormous is Your love for us!

Psalm 8:3-9

> *As one considers Your heavens, O Lord, the work of Your fingers, the moon and the stars, which You have established, what am I that You are mindful of me, a mere son of an earthborn man, that You care for me?*
>
> *Yet You, Lord, have made me a little lower than God, and You have crowned me with glory and honor. You gave us dominion over the works of Your hands by putting all things under our feet; all sheep*

and oxen, the beasts of the field, the birds of the air, and the fish of the sea; whatever has life and breath and passes through the paths of the seas.

O Lord, how majestic, glorious, and excellent is Your name in all the earth!

Psalm 25:8-10

Good and upright are You, O Lord. You instruct sinners in the way, lead them in humble justice. You teach the humble Your way. O Lord, all Your paths are lovingkindness, goodness, truth, and faithfulness.

Psalm 36:5-10

Your lovingkindness and graciousness, O Lord, extend to the skies. Your faithfulness reaches to the clouds. Your righteousness is like the mountains of God. Your judgments are like the great deep.

NAMES OF GOD

O Lord, You are the one and only God who sees and provides all. Praise to Jehovah-Jireh!

Father, You are the perfect God who heals and consummates all. Glory to Jehovah-Rapha!

Yeshua, You are the rod of Moses and our banner who guides all. Splendor to Jehovah-Nissi!

Affectionate Redeemer, You are my God who gives divine peace to all. Tribute to Jehovah-Shalom!

Holy Mystery, You are the Holy One who administers perfect justice to all. Sing hymns of praise to Jehovah-Tsidkenu!

Divine Brilliance, You alone remain the divine shepherd of the flock to all. Praise to Jehovah-Raah!

Lord of all, You are devoted to the flock and attentive to the needs of all. Extol Jehovah-Shammah!

Adonai, You are the Divine Flame who burns away the sin of all. Glory to Jehovah-Mekadesh!

Action Step

Listen to no news today, slow down, and be an admirer of the world around you that God created. Look for His handprint in your day. Be open to conversations to learn something; be receptive to the prompting of the Holy Spirit; be willing to share the love of God when a lost soul crosses your path.

Journal

Record your musings today from your heart and how your day was different. Did you sense your Father's smile today, and memorialize how this day was different?

_____

_____

_____

_____

_____

_____

The Day of the Psalmist

Step 3 / Day 3

A Day of Exploration

TODAY IS A DAY OF EXPLORING AND DISCOVERING WHAT God has beautifully displayed before you. Nature is not only to be marveled at and appreciated, but it also carries a redemptive truth that no man will get away from. A passage that speaks of God's revelation through nature is what Paul writes of in Romans 1:18-21 (NIV).

The wrath of God is being revealed from heaven against all the godlessness and wickedness of people, who suppress the truth by their wickedness, since what may be known about God is plain to them, because God has made it plain to them. For since the creation of the world God's invisible qualities—his eternal power and divine nature—have been clearly seen, being understood from what has been made, so that people are without excuse.

For although they knew God, they neither glorified him as God nor gave thanks to him, but their thinking became futile and their foolish hearts were darkened.

I invite you into our Creator's world. Walking in the glory is to have your entire system cued to the glory. This includes the senses of the body: sight, touch, smell, and hearing. God's

A Day of Exploration

creation stimulates all of these. I noted in my book that in Heaven my senses were in hyperdrive. They have not come down. I do not worship creation as the New Age does, but I worship the Creator, and marvel at the substance of His handiwork. If you take the time and slow down today, you will see the beauty surrounding you.

Following Heaven, I've learned to experience moments during daily life without speaking, just walking with no need for conversation without explanation for silence. Try it today. Experience how comfortable you can be with it, and soon you'll want more. Now that I've started, I can't seem to stop. That's what happens!

Let me tell you that I'm not living at the foot of the beautiful Rocky Mountains, or on one of the beautiful islands of Hawaii, or somewhere in the vast grandness of Alaska. I'm living in the Tri-State area, a short ride from New York City. Yet there is enough beauty to marvel at.

The other day I needed to report for jury duty in Paterson, New Jersey, and there lying on the steps was a lantern fly. I marveled at the creative majesty of God; its colors were amazing.

The point is, nature is divinely arranged. We see it every day; we pass streams, rivers, mountains, pasturelands, and wonderful vistas. Its arrangement of sounds and splendor surrounds us wherever we live. God's handprint is everywhere. "When I look at your heavens, the work of your fingers, the moon and the stars that you have established; what are human beings that you are mindful of them, mortals that you care for them" (see Psalm 8:34). Creation testifies to His existence, as Paul writes in Romans 1:18-21. Consider the following:

Like a window displaying the most incredible pastries, the earth is the stage upon which nature exhibits the handprint of its Creator. If you take the time to explore it, you'll see how everything is incredibly arranged in such artful majestic fashion. It's impossible to walk by in a day without stopping to appreciate it. This is what Heaven did for me that enables me to share it with you. Consider the following.

1. **The Precise Rate of the Earth's Rotation:** If the rotation of our earth had been 1/10 its present rate, the length of our days and nights would have been increased ten times. Our vegetation would burn up during the long days, while the nights would bring such low temperatures that any plant life which survived the day would be sure to freeze.

2. **The Earth Is the Right Size:** The physical size of the earth is just right to support life as we know it. If the earth were as small as the moon, its gravity would only be 1/6 its present force and unable to hold either atmosphere or water. If its diameter were doubled, the force of gravity would be doubled and the atmosphere would be so compressed that its pressure would be increased from 15 to 30 pounds per square inch. This would seriously affect all life. If our earth were increased to the size of the sun, while retaining its present density, gravity would be increased some 150 times. This would increase atmospheric pressure to over a ton per square inch. Life would be virtually impossible under such conditions.

3. **The Earth's Crust Is Just the Right Size:** If the earth's crust had been only ten feet thicker, the metallic elements in the crust would have combined with all the free oxygen in the atmosphere, ruling out the possibility of all animal life. On the other hand, if the oceans were merely a few feet deeper, they would absorb so much carbon dioxide from the air that plants could not exist.

4. **The Moon Is the Right Distance from Earth:** The moon is about 239,000 miles away from earth. If it were only 50,000 miles away, the tides, which are now harmless, would completely submerge the continents twice a day. Though the moon is only relatively close to earth, its surface temperature varies each fifteen lunar days from a high of 214 degrees Fahrenheit above zero to a low of 243 degrees Fahrenheit below zero!

5. **The Composition of the Atmosphere Is Perfect to Sustain Life:** The composition of the atmosphere is about 78 parts nitrogen and 21 parts oxygen. Too much nitrogen in the atmosphere would slow down all functions of the body so that death would finally result. Too much oxygen would also be harmful since it would increase the activities of the body to such a pace that life could not last that long. It is highly unlikely that this could have been developed by accident, since most accidents in chemistry usually result in explosions. This is especially true of nitrogen, which is the basic ingredient of practically every explosive!

6 **The Angle of the Earth Is Just Right for Us to Survive:** The earth is tilted on its axis 23½ degrees. This tilting, plus the revolution around the sun, gives us our seasons. In most parts of the earth this not only gives ample time to raise the necessary supply of food, but it provides a season in which the soil lies idle, soaks up moisture, and increases its own fertility.

7. **The Testimony from the Atmosphere:** The atmosphere of the earth serves a protective blanket to shield us from deadly radiation. If the radiation reached the earth, it would be impossible for humankind to exist. In addition, our atmosphere is just dense enough to protect the earth from some twenty million meteors that enter it daily. These meteors, which travel at speeds of about thirty miles per second, would otherwise strike the earth with such impact that all life would be endangered.[1]

ACTION STEP

Go slow today, and look for things to stop and observe. Discover "uniqueness" and for a few moments be an explorer. If something catches your attention, don't walk by it; stop to give God glory for His creation.

PRAYER

Lord, open my eyes this morning to Your handiwork. Let me see and hear the sights and sounds of Your creative majesty. I thank the Lord for the things You will show me today that have slipped my notice from the busyness of life. Slow me down, Lord, so I may see, hear, and taste Your goodness and learn more of Your presence.

Journal

As in the former day, record your adventure today. List seven things you never noticed and how they increased your admiration for God's handiwork. It could be people, places, or something that you choose. List seven admirations versus seven text messages. Which one is more eternal?

> *Let the words of my mouth and the meditation of my heart be acceptable in your sight, O Lord, my rock and my redeemer* (Psalm 19:14 ESV).
>
> *You make known to me the path of life; in your presence there is fullness of joy; at your right hand are pleasures forevermore* (Psalm 16:11 ESV).

Note

1. https://www.blueletterbible.org/faq/don_stewart/don_stewart_377.cfm.

Step 4 / Day 4

Leaving the Monkey Mind

It is the love of God that feeds our soul. Spiritually, He is sweet to our soul, which brings a fiery warmth to the often bone-chilling coldness of the world. Every day, He offers us a glorious privilege: *"It is the glory of God to conceal a matter, but the glory of kings is to search out a matter"* (Proverbs 25:2 NKJV).

Get kingly.

Get unstuck from your schedule and responsibilities as you find your power. Open your eyes to the God of wonder today.

But how, you ask?

Stop and slow down. Observe what I have created, says the Lord. I am all around you in the light of My glory. Just look.

Too often, life is so intense that one can be like a monkey swinging from branch to branch at full throttle. It takes effort to grab its attention, and force it to focus. When your mind is anxious and racing, when your thoughts are repetitive and unproductive, you feel like you need to press pause but you can't. You're snagged by the world system dictating the way to live. Stop. Slow down.

Once you have jumped out of the monkey mindset, you can begin observing things of beauty in your Father's world today. You'll be prompted to see more.

It's easy to be out of the monkey mindset when relaxing and away on vacation. But it becomes more challenging, and perhaps even more rewarding during your workday, because it takes more effort, discipline, and desperation. Yes, desperation! A necessary quality for transformation and reformation in our lives.

You see, the Spirit wants to animate your soul so that you do all things for the glory of God, whether you eat, drink, or whatever you do (see 1 Corinthians 10:31). The glory has a way of hitting all the right notes, just like the Bible, the book of wonder. Open your eyes today to His wonder. Take nature, another trustworthy source that has three leaves—Heaven, earth, and sea. Heaven is the first and the most glorious, by its presence, we can see the beauties of the other two.

The Bible reminds us that there are many glories to fill our minds. There is a celestial glory and Kingdom—the highest and noblest of the degrees of glory—where God Himself reigns. There is the terrestrial realm. There are terrestrial bodies, not celestial bodies, and they differ in glory as the moon differs from the sun (see 1 Corinthians 15:40). As noted above, *"It is the glory of God to conceal a matter, but the glory of kings is to search out a matter"* (Proverbs 25:2 NKJV). Go out this morning like a king and search them out. Go! Find them! Resolve in yourself to adore God.

Today, practice slower living, stop to breathe slower, and think about the concept of bending the kingdom of the earth toward the Kingdom of God. Look around you and up to the heavens, the clouds and sky. Try marveling at the wonder of God. Don't let the day control you, but control the day from the moment you leave your home. Let the day serve you rather than you serve the day.

ACTION STEP

Stop. Muse over the blessings of the Lord in your life, and be intentional in enjoying God's creation. Resist the monkey mindset that everyone has around you. From the moment you step out of your home, go slow and look around you. Observe those fabulous living things in their unique designs that pass your eye gate daily. Try to see everything through your Father's eyes.

Throughout this day, practice slight humor and a touch of thankfulness. Strive to see everything in the light of eternity to bring levity and wonder into your day.

Stop to experience the sounds passing your ear gate, or a scent that is carried from one place to another.

Stop to marvel at the industry of something as small as the ant, or birds making a nest preparing for their offspring.

Today is a day of discovery. Go out like a king and search them out. Go! Find them! Resolve in yourself to adore God.

PRAYER

Lord, open my eyes this morning to Your handiwork. Let me see and hear the sights and sounds of Your creative majesty. I thank the Lord for the things You will show me today that have slipped my notice from the busyness of life. Slow me down, Lord, so I may see, hear, and taste Your goodness and learn more of Your presence.

Journal

As in the former day, record your adventure today. List seven things you never notice before, and how they increased your admiration for God's handiwork. It could be people, places, or something that you choose. List seven admirations versus seven text messages. Which one is more eternal?

> *Let the words of my mouth and the meditation of my heart be acceptable in your sight, O Lord, my rock and my redeemer* (Psalm 19:14 ESV).
>
> *You make known to me the path of life; in your presence there is fullness of joy; at your right hand are pleasures forevermore* (Psalm 16:11 ESV).

Step 5 / Day 5

APPLYING THE GOSPEL

What does it profit, my brethren, if someone says he has faith but does not have works? Can faith save him? If a brother or sister is naked and destitute of daily food, and one of you says to them, "Depart in peace, be warmed and filled," but you do not give them the things which are needed for the body, what does it profit? Thus also faith by itself, if it does not have works, is dead. But someone will say, "You have faith, and I have works." Show me your faith without your works, and I will show you my faith by my works. You believe that there is one God. You do well. Even the demons believe—and tremble! But do you want to know, O foolish man, that faith without works is dead? Was not Abraham our father justified by works when he offered Isaac his son on the altar? Do you see that faith was working together with his works, and by works faith was made perfect? And the Scripture was fulfilled which says, "Abraham believed God, and it was accounted to him for righteousness." And he was called the friend of God. You see then that a man is justified by works, and not by faith only (James 2:14-24 NKJV).

Life is a process of unfolding pages in a book called life. Years of turning pages, and closing chapters, all filled with experiences. A sacred pilgrimage I will say. Then it happens. We meet the Maker of Heaven who sent His Son for us. Our purpose changes—we hunger to reveal Him in the way we live, showing that God is a Spirit, and we worship Him in spirit, and commune with Him in spirit. Who doesn't need to know this marvelous God?

We learn to love and forgive others. With understanding and God-given empathy, we embrace God's love for others. It's summed up in the word "application." That is why we forgive those who hurt us, because forgiveness and love are the core expressions of the gospel message, and the very application of the gospel. It is in fact a manifestation of His glory.

Question: Are you applying this glorious truth and power throughout your daily life? Are people seeing His glory in and through you? That is the aim of God's children, isn't it? We are called to reflect the divine. If we strive to be present wherever we are, rather than being pulled and pushed by life's current, we experience a greater consciousness of the needs of others, living more duty-bound in sharing the love of Messiah.

The application of the gospel is that we lead others on the same path that we were given.

- Don't hoard the glory—share it.
- Don't just bask in His love—be generous with it.
- Share the love that God gave you. God wants us to be so filled with the Spirit that we forget these things of the earth; we "press toward the mark for the prize of the high calling of God in

Christ Jesus" (Philippians 3:14 KJV), and we see that we have received the life of the Spirit, which has quickened us, for "where the Spirit of the Lord is, there is liberty" (2 Corinthians 3:17 KJV).

Notice the word "liberty."

What kind of liberty?

Liberty that loosens you until you are absorbed in more of His glory. Second Corinthians 3:17 (KJV) states, *"Now the Lord is the Spirit, and where the Spirit of the Lord is, there is freedom."* It is the Spirit, friends, that makes us alive; it is the Word that brings life, and we are to eat of the "hidden manna" (see Revelation 2:17).

Friend, the Spirit breathes; the Spirit lifts; the Spirit teaches; the Spirit renews; the Spirit quickens these mortal bodies; the Spirit enlivens the soul to bring life to a spiritually dead person. How do we live in the place where we say that He can work in us to will and do for His good pleasure (see Philippians 2:13)?

> *I will proclaim your name to my brothers and sisters. I will praise you among your assembled people* (Psalm 22:22 NLT).
>
> *I proclaim your saving acts in the great assembly; I do not seal my lips, Lord, as you know* (Psalm 40:9 NIV).

Action Step

Be intentional in doing things slower today—drive slower; don't keep your foot on the accelerator of your day trying to keep pace with the rest the world. You own the day! Practice application. Look for a lost soul. Look for someone to pray for. Be kind, gentle, and loving. Bend the kingdoms of this world toward the Kingdom of God, by allowing yourself to be bent (used) for His glory—actions, thoughts, and attitudes. Share the good news with others. Determine to be His extended hand of compassion and love.

Would you release the Kingdom of God in you today? Share the gospel with at least three people.

Prayer

Lord, take me by the hand today, and don't let me leave You. I want to walk with You more closely than yesterday and even tomorrow. Lord, help me to be bold in sharing Your love, and fill my heart with compassion for the lost. Let me not fill my days with my pursuits and pleasures, but give me Your heart for those destined to eternal darkness.

Journal

Share how your day was in sharing the gospel. Record how the Lord led you to someone and how you ministered to them. How did it feel?

_____
_____
_____
_____
_____
_____

Applying the Gospel

Step 6/ Day 6

LEARNING SCALES OF IMPORTANCE

I REALIZE IN THIS DEVOTIONAL AND THE BOOK, HOW MUCH I need to talk about the soul. If for no other reason than to provide a release valve for the pressure that's building inside so many.

You see, in contrast to dancing past the darkness, it's impossible to envision how the day will go or end. None of us can. It may not be that charming mixture that you wanted, because the world is an expansive display of cold and harsh realities. Learn to detach from these robbers of time and peace, that are around every corner. Change the subject of your focus and thoughts.

Still, joy can strike your cheeks knowing that every morning is a day filled with good and pleasant surprises. The key is knowing scales of importance: what deserves your attention. Learn to let go of unimportant things so as not to hemorrhage spiritual and emotional power and strength.

Essentially, it is learning to trust more.

The Hebrew word for trust is an action verb *(batach)* and conveys the idea of hope, reliance, and confidence. Its basic meaning is to trust in someone with whom we have confidence. Who is that person? Yeshua, Jesus our Lord. No one is more unswerving in devotion than Him, and you are far more critical to the Kingdom and His plan for you than you think. God is far more involved in your life than you realize.

Don't let people and situations scream for 911 attention. "Please call! It's urgent—I need to know now!" Or a harsh word from someone ignite an internal blaze merely from someone's lack of self-control.

Decide to be your own holy steward of your soul today, by maneuvering your thoughts from moving to sitting. In other words, don't let people or events move you. Bring stillness into your soul, while holding tightly to the reins of your mind and emotions. Don't let the anchor drift. You might feel out to sea amid a tempest, but you are anchored into the bedrock of Jesus. It would be easy to be patient if everyone did everything according to your plans, but the actual test God has given us is abiding in patience and assurance with those people we find so challenging in our lives.

Control the day, don't let the day control you. Choose this day not to react but remain steady and fixed in the love and protection of God.

Action Step

Be mindful of nonessential issues. Not everything needs your immediate attention. Identify those things that can wait, those issues screaming for your attention and demanding your action. Give them no quarter, and separate abstract problems and conversations from concrete things. Focus on what's important. Learn scales of importance! Learn to say no, and let your yes be yes and your no be no.

Prayer

Lord, make me sure of Your love, unmoved by people and situations. Make my feet like iron today, not easily moved by today's events. Give me self-control, and solidarity with knowledge, and help me be unswerving on truth's path. Stabilize my anchor; keep my mind taut in Your hand, Father. Let no person or any thought disrupt my glory mindset of You!

Journal

Record one or two experiences in which you had self-control, and remained strong amid dealing with a person or situation. Write down your testimony of victory over the experience you could have handled differently.

> *Better a patient person than a warrior, one with self-control than one who takes a city* (Proverbs 16:32 NIV).
>
> *We who are powerful need to be patient with the weakness of those who don't have power, and not please ourselves* (Romans 15:1 CEB).
>
> *Do not be anxious about anything, but in everything by prayer and supplication with thanksgiving let your requests be made known to God* (Philippians 4:6 ESV).

Step 7 / Day 7

INSIDE-OUT LIVING

O Lord, Your majestic name fills the earth! And although the earth is darkened and grayed by sin, Your glory is higher than the heavens. When I look out upon the land of confusion, anger, and turmoil, I look at the night sky and see the work of Your fingers—the moon and the stars You set in place. They have never moved from the place You assigned them. From our former days of old and for all our tomorrows, You endure in the place You have set my life.

WHEN YOU LIVE MORE IN THE PRESENT, YOUR SENSES ARE cued inversely (inside-out living); you have a greater awareness of the things and people around you. Let me explain.

When the "outside-in life" is not driving you, moments in a day offer you greater significance, where you find yourself slowing down; the day is not in control of you. This is the genius of inside-out living.

As is well known, each day we walk the same perimeter within our daily routine, rarely jumping out to know the many people navigating the same perimeter. Everyone is crossing the same traffic and parking lots, heading for work, walking swiftly, and running as if everyone is late. People are all around us looking for purpose and meaning to living. They run, but they don't want to run—they wish they could slow down, but they don't know how.

As outside-in living defines most people, be different. Peculiar. Live today inside out. Appreciate the things that most take for granted—those stars in the night sky that are unique and sovereignly positioned by our Creator.

Inside-out living sensitizes you to the Holy Spirit. Things and people formerly unnoticed now slide into your eye gate. Something old becomes a discovery. When you arrive home, you notice that decorative wrought iron like a cluster of stars shining brightly in the evening. You're no longer passing the burning bush and not seeing the fire. I say, step outside yourself and live inside out. Try it today!

Personal Examples

I found that inside-out living increases the activity of the Kingdom in me. As I mentioned in the book, one day I was cued for the Kingdom when a woman with a huge black Newfoundland crossed my path. That day she received the Lord.

I was in line at the food store and was cued to a sad look on a man's face who received prayer in the store. I was in Costco and the cashier seemed to carry a heaviness on his face. He needed prayer, and he got it. Inside-out living is the Holy Spirit repeatedly cueing us to act on our Father's behalf. God will manifest His glory if you are willing to live from the inside out.

Action Step

Invite the Holy Spirit into your morning and ask Him to activate in you today. Nurture a sensitivity to the presence of the Holy Spirit moment to moment. Picture the Holy Spirit in the car, at work, in conversations, and in everyday activities—be mindful of the Holy Spirit, and ask Him today to keep you by His side all day.

Prayer

Lord, let me not be so earthly minded that I am no heavenly good, but let me be so heavenly minded that I am of great earthly good. Help me to have an intimate walk with You today, Holy Spirit, and that I have the sensitivity to Your activity in everything. Holy Spirit, let me know what You want me to see; let me do what You want me to do; show me the way this morning, so that my day follows in the train of Your glory, and my thoughts are never far from You. Show me how to appreciate present moments with You.

Journal

Write down how the Lord directed your steps today to live a more presence-sensitive day. Memorialize the actions and meditations you had today to be more heavenly centered. Determine the following:

- Today my soul won't be shaken by events.
- I won't allow my soul to be overwhelmed.
- I will stop at times, take a deep breath to breathe, and meditate on His love and that His salvation will comfort me.

- I choose to finish this day in both the light of eternity and the glory of His presence.

Dancing past the darkness is a daily dance and starts new every day. Find points of reference in the spiritual realm, so that you can live more spiritually and heavenly centered (see Matthew 6:34). The prophet Jeremiah says:

> *But blessed is the one who trusts in the Lord, whose confidence is in him. They will be like a tree planted by the water that sends out its roots by the stream. It does not fear when heat comes; its leaves are always green. It has no worries in a year of drought and never fails to bear fruit* (Jeremiah 17:7-8 NIV).

Living with Heaven's Glory Mindset

Step 8 / Day 8

Focus on the Potter

But now, O Lord, You are our Father; we are the clay, and You our potter; And all we are the work of Your hand (Isaiah 64:8 NKJV).

WE ARE ALL CLAY IN THE HANDS OF THE MASTER POTTER. Nothing more and nothing less. Yet His fingers are shaping our lives as a Potter shapes the clay. He makes noble and ignoble vessels. Some are broken and used. *"Does not the potter have the right to make out of the same lump of clay some pottery for special purposes and some for common use?"* (Romans 9:21 NIV).

Every vessel of clay, if it could speak wants to be special in some way. Something inside all of us wants to be noticed. We yearn to feel a sense of contribution to the world that makes a difference. But we are always mere clay in our Father's hands, aren't we? And even though we were created with the freedom to make our own moral choices, God does whatever He wills with His creation (see Psalms 135:6; 155:3; Daniel 4:35; Isaiah 46:9-11). O Lord, we are the clay, and You are the potter.

I invite you this morning to meditate upon the following four ingredients that our Father uses in our lives. Each stage

...er bypassed, but its process is greatly accelerated today ...e to the hour that we're in.

Four Ingredients

1. Time: The Process for All

Process allows faith to set things in order. Process is a series of actions or steps taken to achieve a particular end. We understand the importance of process in many areas of our lives, but how about the spiritual side of our lives? Are we aware of the fact that we are in a process daily for God's glory? Process then takes time, because the metal of our lives needs to be refined. For this reason the Bible says not to let a novice teach, because time has not made them ready (see 1 Timothy 3).

Know your time! It's as great a sin to stay in the background when He calls you to the front, as it is to stay in the front when He has called you to the back.

> *The heart of man plans his way, but the Lord establishes his steps* (Proverbs 16:9 ESV).
>
> *So, teach us to number our days that we may get a heart of wisdom* (Psalm 90:12 ESV).

2. Drink: We need to drink.

Inherently, we are thirsty both physically and spiritually. But our drinking is (always) in proportion to our spiritual thirst. Just as we need physical water daily, so too we need spiritual living water. Take the opportunities while you have them to dig your spiritual wells and fill your cisterns. If not, even the simple storms may crack the cistern of your life, and weaken your spiritual life. Incorporate daily reading of the Word of God into your life.

"So my soul pants for You, God. My soul thirsts for God, for the living God; when shall I come and appear before God?" (Psalm 42:1-2 NASB).

Then these familiar words come to us from the Lord in Matthew 5:6 (NASB): *"Blessed are those who hunger and thirst for righteousness, for they will be satisfied."*

3. *Fire: Be Bendable*

Fire and heat make the metal bendable. When metal retains too much spring and hardness, it must return to the fire. Often we follow the same process. Sometimes the Lord makes sudden and strange demands of us when He asks for complete control of our lives, businesses, or the schemes we are presently engaged in. We resist, and need more heat to soften the metal in those times.

Be slow to react.

Don't allow positive or negative circumstances to define what God is doing and how He is molding your life. Be slow to conclude, but quick to let time have its way.

Can we ever really know what our Father is doing in and through us?

God's order of business is to burn off the dross and purify those impurities that find their way back into our hearts. God wants good desires, proper attitudes, correct thinking, righteous actions, and conduct. Work on that today! Be introspective today!

4. *Skillful Hands*

I am more acceptable in Your hands, O Lord.

The word that came to Jeremiah from the Lord: "Arise, and go down to the potter's house, and there

I will let you hear my words." So I went down to the potter's house, and there he was working at his wheel. And the vessel he was making of clay (Jeremiah 18:1-4 ESV).

Picture yourself on a potter's wheel being shaped and molded. You see, everyone has a sense of where they flourish and thrive. God the Master Potter knows this better than we do. Even though we have an inclination of what makes us happy, God knows better. Only in His hands, yielding and cooperating, do we discover our mission in life. Let Him have His way with you today!

"Does not the potter have the right to make out of the same lump of clay some pottery for special purposes and some for common use?" (Romans 9:21 NIV).

Action Step

Can you see what He is working on in your life today? Take the time to see it because it will be in plain sight. Can you visualize where you want to be? Speak it out in words that are audible to your soul. What kind of vessel do you want to be for Him? Less reactive? Not losing self-control or responding to angry people or situations? I want to stay peaceful, Lord, when I encounter rash and foolish people. I want to pray for their salvation!

Prayer

Lord, today You are shaping me again. It is a new day of forming and shaping. Give me the strength to not resist but rest in Your hands as simple clay. You are making me into Your glory.

Let the clay of my life not stand up and fight or question the Potter. Make me pliable and willing today to be Your instrument and vessel.

JOURNAL

Record the security you felt today resting in the Potter's hands. List something that the Potter showed you about yourself today.

Step 9/ Day 9

Learning to Feel Again

I considered the Lord this morning as I lifted my eyes to Him. Before the day even begins, I know that He is the Rock below my feet. Call upon the Lord differently this morning, as one who is worthy to praise Him, and He is worthy of your praise. Yes, you! Whatever the day brings, you can be assured to be unshaken, because you know that you can trust in His steadfast love.

I want you to feel that again today. No more being closed off like a vault door that has been shut up tight due to the hard knocks of life, leaving you in silence and disappointment. This year, the Hebrew year 5783, is a year of liberation and healing for your soul. I want to say that I have no idea where that hurt and pain came from, but He knows exactly what you need in this day and in this season of your life.

Take the time today to study the sky with its unique cloud formations. Feel the ground below you differently than you've ever felt it before. To do this, put aside your problems and needs for today. Don't let your needs and worries disguise your silence; rather, let your silence come from the awe of God's glory. One is negative; the other is positive.

Living Flat

You see, most are naturally oriented to the earthly flat plane of life as we spoke about in the book. I call it horizontal living.

Rarely do we look up unless a meteor is streaking across the sky. Your challenge is to gather spiritual inferences throughout your day, but you'll need to look up often to see more of the world you pass by in a day, because there are many things above and around you that are worthy of your attention. God wants you to feel His presence everywhere in your day.

King David meditates on the heavens, offering beautiful descriptions of God's creation. The language that David uses is that the heavens continuously declare the glory of God (see Psalm 19:1-6). *"Day to day pours out speech, and night to night reveals knowledge"* (Psalm 19:2 ESV). It's as if God's glory is too great to be contained by a single day, so it overflows into the next night, again into the next day, and so on. Whether day or night, you can go outside and look to the heavens as they declare God's glory.

THE HEAVENS ARE PLURAL

David speaks of the heavens, in a plural sense. Why? Because of their variety. Nature is a language of signs by its existence, and for that reason it speaks by actions and operations. No reasonably minded person living beneath the heavens can be without the knowledge of a divine creator (see Romans 1:20). How could someone not look at the night sky and say, "Wow! There must be a great God to have made all of that!"

Part of seeing differently (more with glory eyes) is knowing the difference between earthly time and Heaven's time. Let me explain.

Since my life and death and return to Heaven over two years ago, I never wear a watch. I move according to a daily rhythm and have learned to know the time by the position of the sun. For some that may seem extreme, but I believe it's part of the work of Heaven in me.

As noted earlier, earthly time is horizontal, flat, and limited—hours in a day, days in a week, weeks in a month. Heaven's time is vertical, having depth, and is timeless. There is something to discover every day. As our relationship with God is vertical, He wants to intersect this horizontal, linear life. He wants to slow us down by holy interruptions, like traffic coming to a dead stop. These stops give us more space and time for Him to use us in a day. That's all He wants! Try it, you'll see. He will be there!

As we learned from our *Dancing Past the Darkness* study, horizontal living can be monotonous too. It's compared to a train moving on its track day in and day out, people getting off and on. Rarely does anyone take the time to know someone. Although flat living shares common space with others, as on a bus or train, at church, in a restaurant, or at an event, there is no real interaction.

For 25 years, I commuted on a bus to New York City. Men had identical tan raincoats and carried Samsonite briefcases. I always had an aversion to that. Sometimes it's the way from one generation to the next, as sons follow their fathers. Rarely was time taken to consider something different. In this flat orientation, life is defined by the status quo. But what pleasure, or pleasant trigger, occurs to feel His wonder and glory?

When I returned from Heaven, horizontal living was confining. I needed to live that inside-out conscious life that is filled with divine opportunities. Yesterday on my walk to the grocery store, I felt the leading to stop by a stream to marvel at its clear running water. Then a fabulous crane generally not native to these parts casually strolled out from under the tree-covered waters. I could have walked by in the everyday haste of life and missed it. But God had me stop and linger. I'm living inside out, you see.

Now I can tell you that before my life and death, I limited myself to the external nature of things. We all do it. We don't stop long enough to look beyond the obvious, like a flower's interior waiting to be discovered. We have conversations with people, but their words go in one ear and out the other. The fact is that my senses operated at their optimum in Heaven. On earth, our senses are rarely exercised as they could be. I invite you to let them reward you with more pleasure as God created them.

ACTION STEP

Give God space and time today. That's all He wants! Learn something new today. Perhaps see something old in a new light. Be mindful of the difference between linear and vertical life. Notice how little in a day you look up and how fixed you are on linear vision—how many times someone's words go in one ear and out the other without any consideration of the person. Notice how you pass things without inspection—a beautiful flower, a beautiful tree. Something has entered your eye gate without a pause for further examination.

PRAYER

Lord, let me break from my routine to experience more depth and dimension in Your created things. Help me stop along the way to enjoy the nature surrounding me; help me listen to people's words and not let them go in one ear and out the other. Help me to learn something new today from listening to someone. Help me to see and hear in a new way today.

Journal

Enter into your journal your experience of seeing, hearing, feeling, and learning something new.

Learning to Feel Again

Step 10/ Day 10

Exercise Faith Today

As we sit and watch our prayers rise like incense over our days, we are comforted that there is no god like You. You are truth, love, and hope. You endure beyond time because You have always existed. You are always there as long as morning shines and night ends our days.

As most hub around the darker happenings of a day, reframe your thoughts to boost the goodness of Him in you. Say to yourself that there is goodness in you. Put Messiah's perspective on the world around you too. See through that imperfect glass of the day and focus on the positive.

Today we work on imagining great things again. Go ahead, imagine that prayer finally being answered. Can you visualize it in your mind's eye again? Now wrap faith around those unanswered prayers. But you must visualize it again.

Einstein said about imagination that "[t]he true sign of intelligence is not knowledge but imagination." But faith requires your imagination. Without it faith becomes difficult.

Consider that faith is the substance of something that you hope for, the mark of things unseen (see Hebrews 11:1). And hope needs to be visualized in your mind's eye. Imagination. In other words, God gave us the ability to release those things that are not as though they are. Not for carnal or self-glorifying purposes of course, but for Kingdom importance. This employs the imagination.

- Hope is the belief that your future can be better than your past. This is conceived in your imagination instantly. Then faith is released around it, which can only come through the saving work of God's Son.
- One might hope and believe that a marriage needs to be restored, and you already have it visualized.
- You're hoping for healing and what life will be like when you're whole again.
- I prayed for a man the other day in the marketplace bound to a wheelchair. He asked for prayer to be set free from it; he visualized the liberation that he could have again and he got it.
- What about that financial miracle you have conceived in your mind, believing by faith for it? One sees things that are not as though they are (see Romans 1:17).
- Perhaps a lingering need has become a mountain in your way and your prayers have crashed into the sea of disappointment. The relics of your past have sat before you far too long.

I see someone broken from disappointment who has lost faith. You've shared it for so long that it's a cliché to the point of embarrassment, so you don't share it any longer. Your life feels broken. Stillness often captures your soul, and only the sound of your breathing from the pain can be heard.

In my heart of love, I have compassion for you. I'm sorry for your pain. But I see you raising your hands to trust again, no longer jerking your hands away. I say it is okay. God has come to embrace your heart from the pain, and He is saying it's your time. Imagine God moving in your situation. Exercise your imagination (your vision) and conceive by faith what you hope for. Isn't today the day to return and begin to believe again?

Action Step

Let's exercise our imaginations:

- Imagine for a moment that the love of God is so natural to you that you no longer are doing things to win the approval of others but are living daily without fearing others.
- Imagine being able to trust again, no longer feeling unworthy and useless and unloved.
- Imagine no longer feeling that you don't belong or are unimportant, but now you're free from striving to perform. We welcome the abundant life that comes through our Father's love!
- Picture in your mind's eye that those lost things are being restored. God will compensate you for the years that the swarming locust has eaten—your best years. The creeping locust, the stripping locust, and the gnawing locust will

surrender your destiny and a season of reclamation (see Joel 2:25).

Prayer

Help me, Lord, for my faith to rise again; help me believe in the impossible and that You are my God of all possibilities. In this day, Lord, should You tarry, I will arise again and be called blessed, able, and strengthened by the faith that You have placed with me through the blood of Your Son. Now hope is like a lost treasure rising from within my soul. Let this day be a new day dawning in the face of increasing faith.

Journal

Enter into your journal God's blessing today in your life.

Pleasant words are a honeycomb, sweet to the soul and healing to the bones (Proverbs 16:24 NASB).

And now, dear brothers and sisters, one final thing. Fix your thoughts on what is true, and honorable, and right, and pure, and lovely, and admirable. Think about things that are excellent and worthy of praise (Philippians 4:8 NLT).

Living with Heaven's Glory Mindset

Step 11 / Day 11

Dare to Be Right

In the third year of Hoshea son of Elah king of Israel, Hezekiah son of Ahaz king of Judah began to reign. He was twenty-five years old when he became king, and he reigned in Jerusalem twenty-nine years. His mother's name was Abijah daughter of Zechariah. He did what was right in the eyes of the Lord, just as his father David had done. He removed the high places, smashed the sacred stones and cut down the Asherah poles. He broke into pieces the bronze snake Moses had made, for up to that time the Israelites had been burning incense to it. (It was called Nehushtan.) Hezekiah trusted in the Lord, the God of Israel. There was no one like him among all the kings of Judah, either before him or after him. He held fast to the Lord and did not stop following him; he kept the commands the Lord had given Moses. And the Lord was with him; he was successful in whatever he undertook. He rebelled against the king of Assyria and did not serve him. From watchtower to fortified city, he defeated the Philistines, as far as Gaza and its territory (2 Kings 18:1-8 NIV).

Have you ever met people who are always bent on being right? Many seem obsessed with it. But it's essential to be right in the right things! Isaiah 5:20 (TLB) states, *"They say that what is right is wrong and what is wrong is right; that black is white and white is black; bitter is sweet and sweet is bitter."*

Today, what was right in the past is wrong. What was wrong in the past is right now. Sins practiced today were forbidden in days past and are now called alternative lifestyles. We offend and insult people when we decide to be right concerning biblical principles. But when we insist that we are right, especially in the wrong things, we slam the door on possibilities. Second Kings outlines true success by being right in the right things. Here are quick points to meditate on:

Choose the Right Motive

"He did what was right in the eyes of the Lord" (2 Kings 18:3 NIV). Indeed, it takes daring to square one's life with that which is right in the sight of God and not culture. Life is filled with aberrant truths that have become normalized. Aberrations are visible everywhere. To normalize something is to make it conform to or reduce to a norm or standard. When we normalize such things as perversions as our society does, and it exists long enough, people can become desensitized to biblical principles (those things that are right).

Television openly displays gay and lesbian couples as normal. Let's be clear, any dead or sickly fish can flow as easily with the living, so we must always do what is right in the eyes of the lord. Today, can you identify someone or a situation in your life that is not right in the sight of the Lord and needs to be aligned with God's truth? Are there wrong motives driving your actions? Choose what is right in the eyes of the Lord.

Put Things in Their Right Place

"He removed the high places, smashed the sacred stones and cut down the Asherah poles" (2 Kings 18:4 NIV). Hezekiah noticed there were things that dishonored God so he broke them down and cast them out, then the things honoring God were set up again. But that takes courage! Today we must have courage, and daring, to put things back in their proper place in the context of righteousness and God's Word. It is often uncomfortable. Putting things back in order in our life and family is not easy. We must put things back in their right place for revival fires to burn in us. Look around your family and relationships; are there things that need to be put back in their right place?

Call Things by Their Right Name

"He broke into pieces the bronze snake . . . called Nehushtan" (2 Kings 18:4 NIV). Nehushtan—a piece of brass. Some called it a piece of God and burned incense on it. We see how idolatry is a blind and stupid minister that exalts useless relics to the place of God. Even a silver cross is no better than a brazen serpent if one does not know the Christ of the cross. The worshipers of money, pleasure, or worldly honor are idolaters like those who adored the brass serpent. Can you see something in your life that needs to be called out for what it is? Has sin crept in and found a comfortable place and is no longer called sin? Perhaps in a relationship, a behavior, or something allowed under the guise of some other name? Call things by their proper name. For instance, it you have anger, don't justify it. Call it by its

right name. Unforgiveness? Call it out. Call things by their right name.

Put Your Confidence in the Right Person

"Hezekiah trusted in the Lord, the God of Israel" (2 Kings 18:5 NIV). Hezekiah's revival was a reformation of social and religious reform. The hearts of God's people had gone into oppression and social decline, and they needed a revival to awaken them. Be circumspect this morning. Have you placed your confidence in your job, money, or something other than God as your source of everything that you need?

> *But you shall remember [with profound respect] the Lord your God, for it is He who is giving you power to make wealth, that He may confirm His covenant which He swore (solemnly promised) to your fathers, as it is this day* (Deuteronomy 8:18 AMP).

Walk in the Right Path

"He held fast to the Lord and did not stop following him" (2 Kings 18:6 NIV). Perhaps you have veered into the wrong path in life and the Lord is calling you back to what you know is truth. Perhaps you are backslidden and today is your day of return. Repent today and ask the Lord for forgiveness and enter back upon the path of life that you once cherished and beheld as a daily treasure. Return to the Word of God, the path of life that is a light to our path and a lamp unto our feet. He comes to you this morning, friend, as the Waymaker, the Light bearer, the Lighthouse that is showing you to His heavenly port for rest and healing.

Enjoy the Right Kind of Success

"And the Lord was with him; he was successful in whatever he undertook" (2 Kings 18:7 NIV). According to the world, the end always justifies the means. In the Kingdom, the means are as important as the end. It's the process to the end that is something that God watches how you handle. In this way, you enjoy the right kind of success. Not according to man, but according to the Lord. Work your craft, business, family, and relationships with honesty, integrity, generosity, and compassion. Learn to give and not hoard, bless and not take, steward and not own. Enjoy the right kind of success due to your righteous actions and decisions.

Show the Right Kind of Independence

"He rebelled against the king of Assyria and did not serve him" (2 Kings 18:7 NIV). Being dependent on God can appear as independence or a rebellious spirit to man. But dependency on God is living independent of the fear and praise of man. So have the right kind of independence, but season it with being submissive to every authority under Heaven and living as a peacemaker in all that you do. Hezekiah rebelled against an evil king because of his dependency on the Lord. This boldness and courage enabled him to stand against overwhelming odds and the status quo.

Action Step

Reflect on your life today concerning the seven lessons of Hezekiah's revival. What areas in your life need to be realigned with this pattern of revival? Reflect on the heart of this man, the way he conducted himself. The bold decisions that he took required courage. He always had the tactical advantage because he had courage and daring to be right in the right things.

Prayer

Lord, help me not be worried and consumed with material things, but let me find contentment in Your presence in me. I find an attitude of gratitude for all You have given me. Help me to practice the Kingdom first in my life.

Journal

Dare to Be Right

Step 12 / Day 12

Marks of a Davidic People

Much is said in the Word regarding the character of David. Equally significant today is a cry for such character to emerge within the hearts of God's people. Heaven imprinted my soul with an extra spark, a surplus, a full tank of deep passion for worshiping anywhere at any place. Should a man or woman begin to yield their hearts to God as David did, Davidic markings could imprint the body, and provide the world with more than the traditional images of church and religion.

They need to see a people whose hearts are "full of God," according to the Hebrew word *shalom*.

This morning I want to list five attributes worthy of reflection regarding David—this remarkable man of God is referred to as a man after His own heart.

> *As the rain and the snow come down from heaven, and do not return to it without watering the earth and making it bud and flourish, so that it yields seed for the sower and bread for the eater, so is my word that goes out from my mouth: It will not return to me empty, but will accomplish what I desire and achieve the purpose for which I sent it* (Isaiah 55:10-11 NIV).

First: The mark of a Davidic people deals with our pride.

> *Wearing a linen ephod, David was dancing before the Lord with all his might, while he and all Israel were bringing up the ark of the Lord with shouts and the sound of trumpets. As the ark of the Lord was entering the City of David, Michal daughter of Saul watched from a window. And when she saw King David leaping and dancing before the Lord, she despised him in her heart* (2 Samuel 6:14-16 NIV).

Davidic people are abandoned to their worship, unafraid of what others say. Forget those around you and cast aside your inhibitions! When God's people meet the supernatural presence of God, and the Glory comes in like a wind, it spears our egos, intentions, and agendas. For men, it spears their false image of masculinity. David danced before the Lord with all his might because he arrived at that intersection between the natural and the supernatural presence of God.

Recall, the ark had been absent, maybe too long to remember. The Bible reveals that David forgot what people and leaders often forget—the importance of the presence in our lives. Too often, it becomes ritual, form, and is simply mundane. David knew what it meant to his people, nation, and himself to have the ark and His presence return! Therefore, nothing would take away from his zeal.

This godly king abandoned himself to worship in the presence of all of Israel, allowing his position as king to drift into obscurity.

How much more for you and me as New Covenant believers of noble and royal descent?

Friend, when you are called to the same devotion and abandon as David modeled for us, some will despise your liberty and freedom. It may come from those closest to you, like family and close friends. For David, it came from his wife Michal. Let our response be, *"I will make myself yet more contemptible than this, and I will be abased in your eyes"* (2 Samuel 6:2 ESV).

Second: Davidic people treat the presence/glory with fear.

> *And it was so, that when they that bare the ark of the Lord had gone six paces, he sacrificed oxen and fatlings* (2 Samuel 6:13 KJV).

There is always proper preparation for handling the presence. Undoubtedly, David considered Uzzah's death when trying to bring the ark to Jerusalem on a new cart. (You can read of this in 2 Samuel 6:6.) Knowing that a good man like Uzzah could have ill-fated things occur to him for handling the ark inappropriately is a terror for all. This certainly made an indelible impression upon him because we see David proceeding with a newfound caution; he walked six paces and then sacrificed.

- Six represents human weakness and the fullness of human effort.
- David had finally understood but it came at the expense of a good man. How often we must come to the end of ourselves at the cost of someone else, maybe someone dear to us.

David had to come to the end of himself before taking the seventh step. This seventh step is the most defining of actions in our life. The seventh step is the step of sacrifice, surrender, and absolute vulnerability. It is a place of desperation for divine intervention. The place of total surrender!

Third: Davidic people have innocent hearts.

Davidic people have a childlike innocence. A naïveté defines them within the world around them even amid their enemies. What a refreshing idea in a cynical world such as ours. Is there such a thing anymore?

Anyone following the relationship between Saul and David recognizes Saul's embittered soul toward David. Yet David stood steadfast with an innocent heart while schemes were underway to take his life. We learn that the innocence of heart always puts God at the forefront of our battles. It is He who desires to vindicate and protect us.

The struggle is that people take matters into their own hands, leaving no room for God to move. Are you in such a situation?

Fourth: Davidic people have their affections set on Him and the tabernacle in extravagant ways.

God is looking for an extravagant people whose hearts are set on Him and the tabernacle of His presence. The word "affections" encompasses our heart, mind, goals, and desires. Thus, the affections of God cannot compete with any other affections in one's life. It is not shared with the world's affections like our business, investments, job, position, etc. In 1 Chronicles 29:3, we have a picture of how extravagant David and the people of Israel were toward the house of God:

> *Moreover, because I have set my affection to the house of my God, I have of mine own proper good, of gold and silver, which I have given to the home of my God, over and above all that I have prepared for the holy house* (1 Chronicles 29:3 KJV).

David gave of his wealth—$1,690,000 in refined gold and silver, as well as what would also be millions of dollars in brass, iron, wood, precious stones, marble, and other materials. The results were impressive with this kind of self-sacrificial leadership over the people. The people gave an additional $166,864,320 of gold, silver, brass, iron, and precious stones.

Fifth: The presence destroys your idols.

Are you willing to pay the price?

> *And the Philistines took the ark of God, and brought it from Ebenezer unto Ashdod. When the Philistines took the ark of God, they brought it into the house of Dagon, and set it by Dagon. And when they of Ashdod arose early on the morrow, behold, Dagon was fallen upon his face to the earth before the ark of the Lord. And they took Dagon, and set him in his place again. And when they arose early on the morrow morning, behold, Dagon was fallen upon his face to the ground before the ark of the Lord; and the head of Dagon and both the palms of his hands were cut off upon the threshold; only the stump of Dagon was left to him* (1 Samuel 5:1-4 KJV).

Man is always zealous for the ark of His presence, but the presence comes at a price; it seeks to cut the hands and head off every idol in our life. Its focus is upon religion, control, materialism, and all unconsecrated areas. It is not passive but aggressive. So it is no shock that we prefer not to go the distance.

Would it be in this hour that a people arise with hearts set on the affections of God, a people whose hearts are moved with the extravagance for God's house and His presence without fear of what we might lose?

Action Step

Worship the Lord today throughout the day. Lift your hands to Heaven and give glory to God wherever you are. Consecrate your steps today and fill your day with adoration and worship by setting your affections on Him.

Prayer

Lord, help me worship You today in freedom and abandonment. Let my affections of the world grow dim and my appreciation set extravagantly upon You and Your love for me. Help me to share this love and affection with someone new today.

Journal

Relate your moments of worship and how they made you feel—the closeness that you felt when you were drawn closer to Him, the further away you felt from the worldly things and occupations. Take each of the five mini lessons to reflect on your own life.

Living with Heaven's Glory Mindset

Step 13 / Day 13

Day of Compassion (Making Room for the Glory)

When I turn my ears toward the land and hear man's words, it is a strange sound that I am unfamiliar with and do not recognize. My ears seem to be incapable of hearing them or understanding them. My heart now beats to a different sound, a different voice that I have always known to be true!

Make today a day of compassion in which tolerance and acceptance become your moral compass. Make room for the Glory; get out of its way.

There are many attributes that reflect the Glory, but two sit on top of a hill that pulls people closer: treat each other with respect and equality. All God's children are equal before Him. The color of the skin and the diversity of tongues are more defining of the persistent love and acceptance of God. Heaven is filled with diversity.

Prejudice by nature robs the Glory from the earth, confuses the unsaved, and causes much harm every day to the witness of an all-loving God. Hence, our love and reverence for God are reflected in how we treat one another.

Today, look to be God's extended hand to pray for the sick, encourage someone, and help someone in need. Tune your soul to heavenly cues by looking for divine appointments with someone in need. You'll see them—a look of desperation and fear will be worn on people's faces.

- That woman coming out of the food store spouting off something to herself from an encounter with another angry soul.
- That person who lands full force on the horn of his car, whose voice rises with a sputter of anger and rage.
- The man at the gas station who is yelling at another person with some harsh expletives.

Truthfully, there is nothing to know that we do not already know. People are in need. It is strange how we can stop seeing people who are painfully absent of peace, while we have the power to help them. For this, we do not need a plan but a heart! We don't need to be part of an organization; we just need simple compassion. We don't need a special day; every day is special. We just need our Father's heart. We just need to let go of our schedules a bit.

Action Step

Look for someone you don't know and ask if you can pray for them. Stop, spot, and step into your destiny and start living inside out. Today, allow the Spirit to be your GPS (God's Positioning System). But be ready to stop whatever you're doing and wherever you are going. The Holy Spirit prepares you as you allow Him to intersect your day. So be ready!

Day of Compassion (Making Room for the Glory)

Prayer

Lord, give me Your heart of love for others today to see everyone in the light of Your extravagant love, and help me be Your hand extended today. Make me sensitive to Your voice and lead me into Your glorious Kingdom work today.

Journal

Enter into your journal an individual you touched today with the love of God and memorialize it in your diary so that you can continue to pray for them.

> *Be kind and compassionate to one another, forgiving each other, just as in Christ God forgave you* (Ephesians 4:32 NIV).
>
> *But love your enemies, do good to them, and lend to them without expecting to get anything back. Then your reward will be great, and you will be children of the Most High, because he is kind to the ungrateful and wicked* (Luke 6:35 NIV).
>
> *Put on then, as God's chosen ones, holy and beloved, compassionate hearts, kindness, humility, meekness, and patience, bearing with one another and, if one has a complaint against another, forgiving each other; as the Lord has forgiven you, so you also must forgive* (Colossians 3:12-13 ESV).
>
> *She opens her mouth with wisdom, and the teaching of kindness is on her tongue* (Proverbs 31:26 ESV).

Living with Heaven's Glory Mindset

Step 14 / Day 14

MEDITATE ON HIS POWER

Clouds bring Your glory; rain falls from heaven and waters the earth to give seed to the sower and bread to the eater; night falls as a closing curtain on a stage; morning comes as a new set is made for the next scene to be prepared for the day's adventure. Whom shall I meet today? Whom can I tell of Your love today? What experience lies ahead for me today as I am caught in His eternal hands? They hold me tightly yet gently enough not to crush me. A mere breath blown in anger can level mountains and flood valleys. Yet He has me gently and tenderly in His hands. He is the God of glory; fearful and awesome is He who sits upon the throne far and wide, resting upon the precipice of all things great and small.

AS WE LEARN TO DANCE PAST THE DARKNESS, PICTURE yourself standing at the top of a mountain on a wide patch of flat rock. Far below lies a vast swath of God's people engaged in warfare, fighting the enemy for all the wrong reasons. Often when life's disruptions occur, we are tempted to blame the devil. Or we are tempted to think that our decision to live a presence-driven life is also under siege by the devil. You know, backlash. Assignment against you. Demons sent to torment you. But the answer is none of those. So let's make haste before you draw any more wrong conclusions and get to the root.

Still, you are sitting somewhere lingering, thinking of the events that have just interrupted your daily dance. It can materialize out of thin air from one moment to the next—one phone call or your last text or conversation with someone. You no longer feel that excitement but feel that you went down Alice's rabbit hole trying to find a way out.

But remember how your morning started with that unyielding enthusiasm.

The first place I want to take you is to your authority.

When our Messiah conquered the spiritual realms, we became a New Creation. Immediately we were unbound from the work of the enemy. We experienced an identity transplant analogous to a medical heart transplant. But we also received a new position, adopted into Abba Father's family. Nothing is more transforming than this adoption (see Romans 8:15; 9:26; Galatians 3:26).

We learned from *Dancing Past the Darkness* how our spirit was raised according to Ephesians 2:6 (NIV): *"God raised us up with Christ and seated us with him in the heavenly realms in Christ Jesus."* Essentially, we are now seated in heavenly places with Yeshua. The power of the devil was broken, and we became covered and sealed in the blood of Yeshua.

The problem in our daily lives is not the devil, because by nature, earth is hard and Heaven is easy. The earth will always be hard since the Adamic fall. Every day of our lives, awaiting our last breath, prayer needs will overshadow our lives—physical, emotional, spiritual, financial, family , and marital needs will be present.

Furthermore, life's bruising can only be healed by looking to the one and only Messiah hanging on that crossbeam where His body was nailed. The blood on the crossbeam proves it today, 2,000 years later still flowing and operating. That day His death suddenly impacted the devil and opened the door to our power and authority in Messiah.

So pause for a moment and sit back in a comfortable chair trying to take in what it means to be covered in the blood. I want you to see what happens when believers get the blood and find its power.

The blood has authority over the devil.

> *And they overcame him by the blood of the Lamb, and by the word of their testimony* (Revelation 12:11 KJV).

What does it mean for you to be an overcomer? Share in your journal.

The blood restores fellowship with God.

> *Therefore, brethren, having boldness to enter the Holiest by the blood of Jesus* (Hebrews 10:19 NKJV).
>
> *But now in Christ Jesus you who once were far off have been brought near by the blood of Christ* (Ephesians 2:13 ESV).

What does it mean to you to have fellowship with God through His blood?

The blood heals through the faith in Yeshua.

> *By His stripes we are healed* (Isaiah 53:5 NKJV).
>
> *He himself bore our sins in his body on the tree, that we might die to sin and live to righteousness* (1 Peter 2:24 ESV).

What does it mean to you to know that through the blood your sins are forgiven and you are physically healed?

The blood redeems you.

> *We have redemption through His blood* (Ephesians 1:7 NKJV).
>
> *The law requires that nearly everything is cleansed with blood, and without the shedding of blood there is no forgiveness* (Hebrews 9:22 NIV).

What does it mean to you to live redeemed and cleansed?

The blood gives life.

> *Then Jesus said to them, "Most assuredly, I say to you, unless you eat the flesh of the Son of Man and drink His blood, you have no life in you"* (John 6:53 NKJV).

What does it mean to you to know that blood gives you life every day of your life?

The blood cleanses your conscience.

> *How much more shall the blood of Christ, who through the eternal Spirit offered Himself without spot to God, cleanse your conscience from dead works to serve the living God?* (Hebrews 9:14 NKJV).

> *But if we walk in the light as He is in the light, we have fellowship with one another, and the blood of Jesus Christ His Son cleanses us from all sin* (1 John 1:7 NKJV).

What does it mean to you that your conscience is free of your mistakes of the past, the errors of your present each day?

The blood sanctifies you.

> *Therefore Jesus also, that He might sanctify the people with His own blood, suffered outside the gate* (Hebrews 13:12 NKJV).

What does it mean to you that Jesus sanctified you by His personal sacrifice?

Action Step

Focus on the power of the blood that broke the control of the devil over your life. Try to understand the soul issues in your life. Take the Scriptures below and memorize them, rehearse them, sow them into your soul today, and let them be your only focus of the day. Read them, state them, and proclaim them.

Prayer

Lord, give me a deeper understanding of Your power for today and the understanding of the power of the blood. Help me walk as a victor through the day, as one who has conquered the dark spiritual realms through Messiah's sacrifice.

Journal

Enter into your journal the understanding that you received in the power of the blood of Yeshua and the liberty that He gave you, and answer the questions posed above.

Step 15 / Day 15

DAY OF YOUR SOUL

Holy are You, O Lord, vast and far is Your throne. I rest on the precipice of all things large and small. All governments, kings, despots, and rulers will bow at Your feet. The earth may shake, the mountains may move, the sky will turn ominous, and the sun will turn to blood. Whether it gives light or turns dark, Your throne is far and wide. It rests on the precipice of all things.

THE DEVIL IS A PARODY OF SORTS IN A BELIEVER'S LIFE because his power was broken. He lost the war. So a suitable second part to the previous day's devotion is learning that believers have soul problems, not devil ones. As we learned in *Dancing Past the Darkness*, your soul is your vineyard, and you are the vineyard's caretaker. That was the central purpose of *Heaven's Soul Cleanse* and *A Rabbi's Journey to Heaven*.

Let's refresh our understanding concerning our divine architecture. We consist of a three-part unit of spirit, soul, and body. The simple diagram here illustrates our three operating parts and their interaction. This interaction all happens in the back room.

Nurturing your inner environment today (your soul) is one of the keys to daily living in the glory. Face your soul and confront your actual work. This inner life is referred to in the Great Commandment:

> *Love the Lord your God with all your heart, and with all your soul, and with all your strength, and with all your mind; and your neighbor as yourself* (Luke 10:27 NASB).

Your soul is a silhouette (profile) of your internal state because your soul defines (expresses) who you are and how you live. You are a soul, and your soul is you. With the soul comes a sphere of feelings and emotions that we must learn to manage. That is why the Bible states that *"the heart is deceitful above all things, and desperately sick; who can understand it?"* (Jeremiah 17:9 ESV), and *"Whoever trusts in his own mind [soul] is a fool, but he who walks in wisdom will be delivered"* (Proverbs 28:26 ESV). One is natural and the other is supernatural.

As the eye is a window into the soul, the same idea is expressed in Matthew:

> *The eye is the lamp of the body. If your eyes are healthy, your whole body will be full of light. But if your eyes are unhealthy, your whole body will be full of darkness. If then the light within you is darkness,*

how great is that darkness! (Matthew 6:22-23 NIV).

ACTION STEP

Look into a mirror this morning and say, "I am a soul; my soul is me. I am also a spirit living in a biological body, moving, and expressing the heart through the soul and physical body. Oh soul, worship the Lord today, and be a blessing!"

PRAYER

Lord, activate in me today so that my soul does not gravitate toward the things of the world. Help my soul stay in contact with the Spirit so that I resist the world's ways today. Let Your love be like a coin in my pocket held tightly in my hand. Let Your Spirit not intone in a low voice but one that registers clearly in my ear today.

JOURNAL

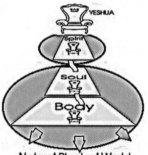

Explain in your journal the four influence centers in the illustration that affect your daily life and how you must steward your soul. Enter your experience today about caring for your soul. Relate how you cared for it in certain circumstances and what it taught you about your daily relationship with the Lord.

Troubled. Fearful. Worried.

My soul is also sore vexed: but thou, O Lord, how long? (Psalm 6:3 KJV).

Listening to his mind, soul, thoughts.

How long shall I take counsel in my soul, having sorrow in my heart daily? How long shall mine enemy be exalted over me? (Psalm 13:2 KJV).

Conviction. Remorse. Guilt.

I said, Lord, be merciful unto me: heal my soul; for I have sinned against thee (Psalm 41:4 KJV).

Disquietness and trouble in his soul.

Why art thou cast down, O my soul? and why art thou disquieted in me? hope thou in God: for I shall yet praise him for the help of his countenance (Psalm 42:5 KJV).

Hopeless. Depressed. Disturbed.

Why, my soul, are you downcast? Why so disturbed within me? Put your hope in God, for I will yet praise him, my Savior and my God (Psalm 42:5 NIV).

Depressed. Fearful.

O my God, my soul is cast down within me: therefore will I remember thee from the land of Jordan, and of the Hermonites, from the hill Mizar (Psalm 42:6 KJV).

Day of Your Soul

Step 16 / Day 16

Learning the Principle of Yield

The principle of yield is repeated 25 times throughout Leviticus. Where the land yields its fruit, the laborer is to yield his work. But the principle of yield equates to advancement too, and often it precedes surrender. The connection between the two is essential.

In a Shemitah year for instance (a sabbatical year that was observed in biblical times), the land was to rest for one year so that another seven-year productive cycle could yield a healthy crop.

Spiritually speaking, seasons of life come when we must stop and yield to harvest fresh understanding to find a way forward. Of course, we can work directly through these, just like the farmer can continue planting and harvesting. But just as the farmer will strip the land of its vital nutrients, so too we can lose the knowledge for something ahead. Perhaps it's the next wilderness or the next mountain to overcome. We can miss fresh understanding.

Lessons from the Wilderness

At this point, we would agree that wilderness experiences can be life-altering; we all get them, and we all successfully come through them. But they can be like a finger pressing intensely against us. Circumstances come into our lives that are not left solely to our Father to work out too. God supplies our needs but He does not make the bread. Natural processes come to bear through divine laws—like rain and sun and harvest, to nurture the seed so a plant is born to give grain to the harvester. Daily we must be disciplined to work in the field of our lives.

Throughout our lives, we acquire a steadiness to face our future. Time allows this. We need those mountains to move, or we need to go through them, or we need to climb them or go around them. Many such seasons can seem unbearable, and we long for a way out. Times such as these come when the most resounding groans emanate from your spirit because you cannot understand life's twists and turns.

But the way is always through. Perhaps God wants us to build a wall afterward. Are you ready to hold the sword and the trowel? (See Nehemiah 4.)

Are you prepared to fight for it as Abraham needed to wave off the birds of prey? (See Genesis 15:11.)

God may call you into full-time service, but are you ready to show yourself approved? (See 2 Timothy 2:15.)

Are you prepared for the pressures of full-time service? (See 1 Timothy 2:12.)

Will you contend or gracefully allow providence to work? Jesus said,

> *Therefore everyone who hears these words of mine and puts them into practice is like a wise man who built his house on the rock. The rain came down, the*

streams rose, and the winds blew and beat against that house; yet it did not fall, because it had its foundation on the rock (Matthew 7:24-25 NIV).

Repeatedly, Moses is a study of victorious living. Numbers 12:3 (NIV) states, *"Now Moses was a very humble man, more humble than anyone else on the face of the earth."* Moses's form of leadership was one that he did not choose. He knew that he was assigned a role because he was simply God's follower and was given a monumental task that needed to be fulfilled. From Moses, we learn that anything of any value takes time and comes with a cost.

We return to this formula of what it takes to become clay—time, water, and the work of fire on our life. Moses was such an individual that he finally reached that stage. When Moses failed to provide meat for his people, he asked God to take his life. In response, God provided 70 elders to share the burden.

No doubt, Moses's view of leadership is rare today. He saw himself not as a CEO, CFO, or president but as a mere operations manager of what God presented to him. He constantly pushed honor away, and he never overshadowed who was ultimately responsible—God.

In our modern day, people gravitate toward those on the grand stage. They cannot wait to be on Facebook with them. Fame and notoriety pulsate in society today. It also spills into the family of God, where people care little about how leaders have managed or mismanaged their lives. I also believe there are many Moses types today—those who have come victoriously through wildernesses of diverse kinds. They have successfully managed their lives, marriages, and families and have withstood the temptations. Their feet have become like iron amid war and made sure they were not easily moved from Him who is above all.

So what is suitable for most speaks loudly of Moses's life. How we have lived our life gives us the ability to scale and measure our character throughout our lives. Only then can we discover the kind of man Moses became.

THE WILDERNESS AGAIN

Moses endured two wilderness experiences. The first was when he escaped Egypt, when he remained in the desert for 40 years. The second came because of the spies' lousy report. Again, another 40 years of wandering would follow.

Learning that we do not always have the answers, sometimes we can only see one step at a time. When those seasons arrive, I have found that our Father does not impose Himself harshly upon us either; He knows when to lay hold of us or leave us alone. He knows something significant is occurring in us.

When studying Moses's life, we discover an essential refining for all. I call it the willingness scale; it measures how much of our lives we are willing to yield to our heavenly Father. How much are we like clay? You know, pliable. How much of the water of the Holy Spirit is found in this earthen vessel so we can be shaped by His hands? Moses seemed to show no bounds.

When Moses finally reached the borders of the Promised Land the second time, he discovered that he would not cross over. Why? For one infraction. He lost his temper in striking the rock for water rather than speaking to it (see Exodus

17; Numbers 20). Yet Moses endured constant struggles with his people from Egypt to Sinai. Then he went into a wilderness for 40 years with more challenges. He battled his internal enemies and provided food for his people and dealt with mass revolt.

But in all the unbelievable images formed in our minds of God's activities through him, Moses was a man deeply held in the Potter's hands. Jeremiah sheds similar light: *"Can I not do with you, Israel, as this potter does?"* (Jeremiah 18:6 NIV). Presented is something that God offers to all who have a willing heart. This will be crucial for the days ahead: "Can I not do with you, My bride, as the Potter desires?" declares the Lord.

Our Lesson

As God drove Israel from one place to the other and scattered them amongst the nations from one corner of the earth to the other, so it is with us. God is in control.

Can you be comfortable with that?

Can you be satisfied with these words: "Can I not do with you as I desire?" declares the Lord?

To experience an adventure with God again, we must let the Potter have His way with us. This comes only from a relationship between the Potter and the clay—we to our Master Potter and Lord.

Action Step

Find a peaceful, quiet place today to allow the Lord to draw you near to Him and raise your awareness of His love, which bears the forgiveness of sins, as you walk in love. Take hold of little solitudes today to reflect on your own life being stretched, formed, and shaped for His glory.

Prayer

Lord, give me the patience to cooperate with You today; let me be open to Your guidance, the light of Your presence. Shine upon me today and bless me with discernment and righteousness, tempered with mercy, that Your grace is sufficient for me on this day. Lord, keep me in Your care as I live and move in Your being. Guide me from error today and direct me from harm's way.

Journal

Enter in your journal your time of solitude with the Lord today. What did you have to do to make that time? What did the Lord speak to your heart, and how was the experience of feeling His love again?

Living with Heaven's Glory Mindset

Step 17 / Day 17

ADOPTION AND SONSHIP

But when the fullness of the time had come, God sent forth His Son, born of a woman, born under the law, to redeem those who were under the law, that we might receive the adoption as sons. And because you are sons, God has sent forth the Spirit of His Son into your hearts, crying out, "Abba, Father!" Therefore you are no longer a slave but a son, and if a son, then an heir of God through Christ (Galatians 4:4-7 NKJV).

IF WE ARE TO RELEASE A STREAM OF A GLORY REMNANT inexorably, we can ask people how much they truly understand about being God's child. How well a person understands adoption will determine if they discovered the foundation of Christianity itself.

Bent on untangling the often-frayed heart of life, God's purpose was to create a genuine feeling of filial love in us. This term is special—love derived from the Latin *filius*, meaning "son," and *filia*, meaning "daughter." It assumes the relationship of a child or offspring to a parent and is at the heart of the spirit and work of adoption.

I often wonder what it would take to see each other as children in the same family.

When I was in Heaven, there was only perfect love, harmony, and unity. These powerful words in our opening passage leave us with a profound mystery, even though it's one of those crown jewels of the gospel message—adoption (see Hebrews 2:3).

> When we are born again, something wonderful happens! Our heavenly Father adopts us with all the rights as His children!

Contrary to our modern-day culture, adoption in Bible times wholly recognized the child as a natural-born heir of a family, bringing us back to filial love.

When Moses was relinquished as a baby, he was given all the rights of an Egyptian; Ruth, as an adult, took on the identity of the Jewish people (see Ruth 4:13,14-16); Bilha, Rachel's servant, was given to Jacob to bear him a child (see Genesis 30:4-6). So adoptees gained all the rights of legitimate sons and daughters of a new family in biblical times.

Similarly, God's children need to cherish the treasure of our Father's choice when He received us. Galatians 4 states that He first knew us. He chose us. We did not choose Him. Yet many struggle to accept the Father's love; so many attempts to find it go on in the wrong places.

Beloved, Yeshua is wonderfully the Way for us all! He is also the key to the front door of Abba's house, where we find our place of refuge. In this, adoption is systemic, complete, and whole! Here are more benefits of adoption in God's family:

1. Adoption brings freedom.

Freedom is being genuinely freed from the bondage of unhealthy expectations from family members, friends, and former thinking patterns. Your identity comes from within, not outside. Paul addresses this from another perspective in Romans 6:4 (NIV): *"We were therefore buried with him through baptism into death in order that, just as Christ was raised from the dead through the glory of the Father, we too may live a new life."* Our old self has died! Of course, this level of transformation depends on how much of our old patterns we are willing to abdicate to our Lord.

2. Adoption gives the courage to apologize.

In actuality, humbling yourself draws pleasure from God—and I'm not referring to the "false" humility rooted in pride. Yeshua's most significant attribute is humility. God is pleased by our willingness to be defined by it. Humility allows these God-centered characteristics to take root in our lives and flourish (see Matthew 5:9). As sons and daughters of God, we gain the courage to say "I'm sorry" or "I forgive you" because humbling ourselves is no longer an assault on our self-worth or pride. Even if we are a fool in others' eyes and are misunderstood, we remember who loves and accepts us! This traces back to the first benefit—freedom.

3. Adoption provides a healthy self-image.

A healthy self-image protects our soul even amid slander, gossip, and character attack. It's not that we don't hurt, because God created us as complex emotional beings. But no one can pull down our self-worth because it is rooted in our position in Christ. Knowing our work, then, is vital to our self-esteem, emotionally and spiritually. See God's power formula at the end. I call it a divine equation for God's people.

4. Adoption brings discipline and a life of submission.

These two are not readily associated with God's love because our human nature hates them. The actual purpose of discipline is freedom. To some, this may seem contradictory. But freedom is the ability to lay down the tiring burden of always needing to get our way. True freedom is also the discipline of submission to God's Word. To the world, of course, this is strange fire. To the family of God, this personal discipline of submission allows us to let things go and leave matters in our Father's hands, of which the world knows nothing.

5. Adoption gives the power of self-denial.

Self-denial is not surrender, compromise, or weakness. It's learning the scales of importance. Some things are just more important than others. A child of God must always know what is most important in any situation. For instance, Yeshua did not fight every person who contended with Him. The wisdom revealed to Him was the scales of importance. We must choose our battles. This is called discernment—knowing the difference! These benefits come to us as sons and daughters of God and are where proper security is discovered.

God's Power Formula for Self-Esteem

Adoption = Position. When one is adopted, they are given a new position in a family with a new future. The past is no more.

Position = Security. When one receives their new position through adoption, they find a new security and love as they become as a natural born heir of a family—no longer feeling second rate but brought up to the front of the line, secure in their new position.

Security = Power. Power comes from the position and security that provide true self-esteem and dignity; it brings the confidence as a new creation. In this way power is derived from position, which provides security and confidence.

We are all adopted into a position as a child of God and heir of the Most High. Herein is the key to abundant living. No one can earn it, and no one has the power to weaken it or take it!

Journal

LIVING WITH HEAVEN'S GLORY MINDSET

Step 18 / Day 18

RIGHT PERSPECTIVE

PERSPECTIVE IS EVERYTHING IN LIFE. TODAY IS A DAY OF new perspectives. So important is this subject that one processes various points of view through it. Often, once we have our point of view, it's tough to change our minds because we get a soldier's mindset.

For instance, my experience with the second heaven, where demons reside, changed my perspective on the devil and his demons. I gained new knowledge. Heaven changed my perspective on almost everything—in areas of prayer, spiritual warfare, and the soul. Heaven radically transformed my outlook on life due to a new knowledge base and experience.

Today's reading challenges us to reframe our thoughts.

Consider two believers: One seems blessed and everything seems to go the right way, while for the other almost nothing goes right. Yet God is the same for both. While in America blessings abound, somewhere else in the world there is abject poverty, dire hardship, and persecution.

Does God intervene in every tiny detail of your life?

Does God answer the prayers of the one and not the other?

A challenging perspective is to see trials and tribulations as blessings because they urge us to grow and develop into more robust, patient believers. I chose to believe God loves me in all situations, not because all my prayers are answered, but because they're not. Not because all my dreams have been fulfilled, but because they're not. Not because one seems blessed and the other is not. God's love over one or the other is no greater or smaller. God also loves the sinner but hates the sin. God loves LGBTQ people, as well as those fighting for abortion rights. All have sinned and fallen short of the glory of God (see Romans 3:23).

What is perspective?

First, perspective requires us to often view things in the light of someone else's situation and experiences. Consider the Holocaust in light of this definition. The most frequent question that Jewish people ask when hearing the gospel is, "If God is all-loving, explain the Holocaust." Such a historical perspective is an uneasy mountain to climb, including the history of antisemitism in the name of Christianity.[1]

If areas of knowledge drive perspective, then what is knowledge? Knowledge can be summed up into three types: explicit (documented information), implicit (applied information), and tacit (understood information). These three elements form a broad or narrow view of life because our perspectives can entrap us, unable to see the other side or beyond it. The Bible, for instance, is explicit, implicit, and tacit. It is the truth and path of life to grow and fulfill our purpose in life.

But what if the truth is not just a point of view?

What if the truth is not just a list of rules—your truth or anyone else's?

What if the truth is not the ever-changing crowd consensus but a Person you get to know and who knows you? This person's story is told in the Bible. His name is Yeshua, the Jewish Messiah.

Perspective can also become one's scales:

- The scales of unbelief
- The scales of tradition and convention
- The scales of familiarity (Yeshua could not perform miracles in His hometown.)
- The scales of religion
- The scales of arrogance foster ignorance.
- The scales of intellect prevent the childlikeness of simple belief at times.
- The scales of experience, thinking that we now know it all
- The scales of age where we are blind to the anointing of the young who are naïve enough to believe what we no longer believe
- The scales of intimidation that blinded Saul to young David

How you see the house of God is determined by your perspective. Ezra 3:12 (NIV) illustrates this principle:

Many of the older priests and Levites and family heads, who had seen the former temple, wept aloud when they saw the foundation of this temple being laid.

Go ahead! Try this perspective exercise. Ask your present elders what America was like only a few decades ago. Then ask long-time believers what the house of our Father was like only three decades ago. Brace yourself for the answers to both. Those who experienced the former glories see it differently than the younger generation. The Bible says that the latter glory will be greater than the former (see Haggai 2:9). This is yet to come!

Action Step

Today, work at seeing the world through the lens of objectivity, of the Kingdom, and in the light of eternity. Identify temporal perspectives that have no bearing on the Kingdom, let alone eternity. Identify those perspectives that need to change for you to be more open. Try to understand someone's point of view in light of their experiences to understand why they feel the way they do and react the way they do. What perspectives have locked you in that you need to be freed from?

Prayer

Lord, show me Your perspective on this day. Help me recognize the work You are doing for me and the sacrifices You make. Help me see a Kingdom perspective on the world around me in my experiences and interactions with today's people. Please help me walk in knowledge and understanding and allow Heaven to change my view of my life. Let me not be soulish, but rather walk in the Spirit by the Spirit and in the anointing of the Spirit.

Journal

Make a list of those perspectives in your life that may need to change. Have you found self-imposed limits in them due to past experiences? People can become prejudiced due to a negative experience. Can you identify such areas in your life?

For My thoughts are not your thoughts, nor are your ways My ways," says the Lord. "For as the heavens are higher than the earth, so are My ways higher than your ways, and My thoughts than your thoughts" (Isaiah 55:8-9 NKJV).

Remember the former things of old, for I am God, and there is no other; I am God, and there is none like Me, declaring the end from the beginning, and from ancient times things that are not yet done, saying, "My counsel shall stand, and I will do all My pleasure" (Isaiah 46:9-10 NKJV).

Note

1. To understand more, see www.metrojewishag.org.

Step 19 / Day 19

Safe-Haven Moments

When I returned from death, I received a solution to daily pressures and to mitigate the glory robbers. It is called "safe-haven moments." I stop and remember that my true home is not here. I am a journeyman visitor with a glory message on my back.

For God's people, a life too deeply entrenched in the world is destructive. The world is dominated by the prince of the power of the air, and therefore is deeply flawed. I have a picture of satan in the bleachers applauding as God's people are racing round and round each day. It will keep you so occupied and distracted that safe-haven moments are impossible to experience. When the glory wants to break out, you are too busy.

You need little solitudes today—time spent with Him along the way to renew yourself in a day—but you say that you have no time. When you need a time of quiet meditation and musing in your day, it's impossible to dial down the noise. Jesus often went away to spend quiet time with our heavenly Father to reenergize, refresh, and renew. In the New Testament, Yeshua spent time alone with the Father many times, as described in these Scripture passages: Matthew 14:13; Mark 1:35; 6:45-46; 14:32-34; Luke 4:42; 5:16; 6:12; 9:18; and John 6:15.

As I have begun to adjust back to mortal life, I stop to remember that my true home is not here. I look up to the heavens regularly to remember where I was. Then I reset myself again.

Today, take time to stop for a deep breath. Gaze up to the heavens, recalling that Heaven is just behind the clouds, where He sits on His throne overseeing your life. Recall that your every day rests under His watchful eye, and His Son is sitting next to Him as your High Priest. Can you visualize your future eternal home nested in an incomprehensible glory?

Stop to invite Him into your situation.

Safe-haven moments are those moments that allow you to string them together in a spiritual mapping that builds a new inner disposition.

I stop to appreciate His handiwork; it's everywhere.

I stop to listen to people's words; I learn something in a day.

I no longer race through my day, because I want to capture all the opportunities. For anytime that occurs, a heavenly flow begins where you again sense His glory presence. This refreshes your soul. Friend, I encourage you to take these safe-haven moments. But you must be intentional. Stop long enough to listen to and observe the world around you; you will find God's handprint everywhere.

You'll need to employ safe-haven moments when you begin your dance past the darkness.

When You Start

When you launch your dance past the darkness, you'll feel that you are entering a new epoch in your day. Visualize it being played out on a Broadway stage and you're in the first row of your life. If the scene had a name, it would be "A New Shangri-La Period" or epoch about to begin. After all, my promise is that you can live under an open Heaven with His glory every day and return to Kingdom normalcy.

But no sooner than the morning begins, a glory robber shows up. It wasn't there an hour ago. An hour ago you were filled with enthusiasm and excitement. What do we learn? Beware of many people who are glory robbers, to situations that are acutely averse to the glory in your day. These joy robbers abound.

How to Respond

Without meandering too far, how will you respond when the light of that spiritual moonbeam is interrupted and disrupts your footing? In all truth, I'll tell you what I do: I steward my soul. I tell my soul to worship the Lord and I force the Word of God upon it. *"Bless the Lord, O my soul; and all that is within me, bless His holy name!"* (Psalm 103:1 NKJV). Then I watch a heavenly flow begin where I sense His glory presence again. I choose the better in my day.

If it's not a genuine 911, let the phone ring. If it's a so-called emergency from work, it can wait. The screaming demands of children (within reason) or spouse can wait. You'll be surprised to discover how many things can wait. You can stop most things, I've found. You'll also find that everything feels more solid while the chaotic world is swirling around you, but you're untouched by it.

Proverbs 18:24 says that the Lord is a friend who sticks closer than a brother. I sense that closeness more than ever now in *Dancing Past the Darkness*. Like a close friend who slung his arm around my shoulder and said, "Let's leave this place of death and darkness," He took me to Heaven and back. Yes, my friend, He is closer to you than a brother. He also wants to be your friend. He wants to wrap His arms around you so that you can lean back and savor moments with Him, allowing your soul to be lifted in your day. He is the lifter of your head! (See Psalm 3:3.)

> Essentially, by taking safe-haven moments, you reset yourself. You're creating life-giving choices that imprint your soul with this spiritual mapping and building a presence-driven life.

Action Step

Today, look to take some safe-haven moments when you remember that this world is not yours. Stop to invite the greatness of God into your time. You have time in your hands. Take it. Take a deep breath. Gaze up to the heavens from time to time to remember that Heaven is just behind the clouds and He sits on His throne overseeing your life. Your every moment is under His watchful eye. His Son is sitting next to Him as your High Priest. At that moment, you can picture your future eternal home of incomprehensible glory. Stop to invite Him into your day and situation.

Prayer

Lord, help me see You in Your majesty and perfection. Be the lifter of my head today and draw my soul upward to heavenly things. Let me not obsess or worry but remember that You are my haven and rock in the tempest of life.

Journal

Can you list three times in your day when you stopped for a safe-haven moment? What was the circumstance?

Living with Heaven's Glory Mindset

Step 20 / Day 20

Issues of the Heart

But mark this: There will be terrible times in the last days. People will be lovers of themselves, lovers of money, boastful, proud, abusive, disobedient to their parents, ungrateful, unholy, without love, unforgiving, slanderous, without self-control, brutal, not lovers of the good, treacherous, rash, conceited, lovers of pleasure rather than lovers of God—having a form of godliness but denying its power. Have nothing to do with such people (2 Timothy 3:1-5 NIV).

Society is suffering from a famine of goodness in people as we have arrived on the edge of end-time changes. The above passage warns us of rapid-fire changes coming with intensity and saturating society. All of this can be boiled down to the issues of people's hearts. Second Timothy 3:1-5 is not untruthful about God's people losing goodness; they will have a form of godliness but deny its power. Behind all the worldly problems, the people of God are trying to thread the needle between these worldly changes and pressures and issues in their hearts. But what is genuine goodness? Authentic goodness is supernatural as it always reveals the heart's spiritual condition.

In Hebrew, "good" is *tov* and means "well done; to be pleasing." Abraham illustrates this beautifully, because Abraham was able to turn over his evil inclinations to God due to the God-centered condition of his "good" heart. He therefore became the father of faith for all (see Genesis 15:6; Romans 4:3) and was credited by God, and called it righteous.

Pure goodness then begins with the expression of God. It expresses itself in loving kindness and mercy. Without God, goodness is unreliable, untenable at best.

For instance, God transforms bad-hearted people and tempers their evil inclinations toward good desires. Lawless individuals become submissive, and hardened people become tender. Good traits emerge that the world is desperate to experience. Perhaps the psalmist had this in mind in Psalm 34:8 (NIV): *"Taste and see that the Lord is good; blessed is the one who takes refuge in him."*

Genuine goodness, then, always traces back to the motivation of our hearts. However, kindness and compassion do not necessarily mean that our hearts are right either. Or does it? What inspires such differences?

Two Approaches

There are two different approaches and motivations for goodness. A rich and famous person can be known for doing good humanitarian deeds, but when they receive accolades and awards from man, how does this fit into God's goodness (see Matthew 6:5,18)? Take a politician who is running for office and comes to a community to make a speech. The next day, they run to get the newspapers to see what kind of impression they made.

They want to see words of praise, right?

Do they want recognition, or do they want to honor?

They want both. They are seeking not only praise but also validation from the public.

But how does this fit in with God's view of goodness?

- God says, "When you fast, do so in private and make sure that you look refreshed" (see Matthew 6:16-18).
- God says, "When you pray, pray in the closet to not look self-righteous" (see Matthew 6:6).
- God says, "When you give, do not let the left hand know what the right hand is doing" (see Matthew 6:3).

If you love those who love you, what credit is that to you? Even sinners love those who love them. And if you do good to those who are good to you, what credit is that to you? Even sinners do that. And if you lend to those from whom you expect repayment, what credit is that to you? Even sinners lend to sinners, expecting to be repaid in full. But love your enemies, do good to them, and lend to them without expecting to get anything back. Then your reward will be great, and you will be children of the Most High, because he is kind to the ungrateful and wicked. Be merciful, just as your Father is merciful (Luke 6:32-36 NIV).

In other words, people should not do things for the praise of others or to look spiritual. Goodness should flow from the goodness in our hearts through the Lord's redeeming work, for out of the heart flow the issues of life (see Proverbs 4:23).

Action Step

Look today to do something for the Lord privately and tell no one about it. Are you willing to bless someone when only you and the Lord know about it? This pertains to giving, praying, encouraging, edifying, and even winning someone to the Lord.

Prayer

Lord, let no praise of man motivate me but only Your glory. Let all that I do for You be held in the secret place and that goodness would flow from my life, not to be seen or heard, Lord, but just to give You pleasure. Lord, keep my heart on serving You and You alone.

Journal

Share in your journal an act of goodness and kindness that no one knows about.

Issues of the Heart

Step 21 / Day 21

SIN OF THE GOLDEN CALF

ONE OF THE GLOOMIEST DAYS IN JEWISH HISTORY OCCURRED when the character of one of Israel's most influential men, Aaron, collapsed.

Here is the back story.

Moses was on Sinai getting the tablets from God. But because he was delayed in coming down, many thought that he was taken to Heaven in a chariot. In response, the Israelites demanded a new god. "Rise and make us a god that will be before us," said the people to Aaron. "As for Moses, who brought us out of Egypt, we know not what has become of him" (see Exodus 32:23).

Regrettably, Aaron accommodated the Israelites and asked them to hand over their gold earrings to make a golden calf. Enthralled with the obsession to worship an object, the Israelites and Aaron lost their minds.

The incident of the golden calf was not novel. Israel's warrior-judge Gideon refused Israel's demands to be their king but told them to give him their gold earrings instead. Following this request, he melted down their gold to make a golden ephod and then displayed it in his hometown of Ophrah. That idol too became a snare, and Gideon and the people prostituted themselves, as seen in Judges 8:24.

The moral of this story is that even God's people can lose their minds and do unimaginable things. And then to what enemy do we credit Aaron's fall from grace?

THE ROOT SIN

Aaron was the victim of a chameleon attack—that little innocuous creature that changes its color and character under pressure. It can be challenging to shake it off, as we have all experienced in life to one degree or another. Aaron lost his mind when a strong character was needed. It also revealed the Israelites' sheer ingratitude, ignorance, stupidity, and utter contempt, let alone Aaron's folly, to be swept into this scheme. We don't want to be unfair to Aaron either. Israel got the better of him, as circumstances can get the better of us too!

We need more information. Moses's name in Hebrew is *da'at*, which connotes knowledge. You see, Moses became Israel's source of knowledge. When he was delayed in coming down, Israel felt disconnected from knowledge when they thought he would never return. As fear set in, they attempted to create a new source of knowledge—so their emotions began to rule the day. When Moses returned, Aaron provided a ridiculous excuse: "I simply threw the jewelry into the fire and out came the golden calf" (see Exodus 32:1-6).

After spending two decades in gold refining and manufacturing, I assure you that clear foresight, planning, and model making are required. This was a preposterous notion. However, the sin of the golden calf highlights a more general thesis that concerns our human nature: People operate differently under certain circumstances, and our imagination can also get the better of us. Boy, we have all been there when the imagination rules the day!

Lesson Learned

Any situation can get out of hand through an irrational filter of emotion and imagination. These episodes are often caused by incomplete knowledge. It characterizes the many conflicts in the family of God.

When truth is not present and communications are broken off, the mind can make false associations, where misconceptions of reality occur. This is the lesson of the sin of the golden calf. We should never forget this principle: The truth always illuminates the soul's path and produces genuine emotions and actions.

Paul addresses this in 2 Corinthians 10:5 (KJV): *"Casting down imaginations, and every high thing that exalteth itself against the knowledge of God, and bringing into captivity every thought to the obedience of Christ."* Paul is motivated here by a deep love for the family of God. He wants good-hearted motivations behind our actions and despises hypocrisy, falsehood, and false forgiveness of people.

Consider these additional words from Psalm 15:2 (KJV): *"He that walketh uprightly, and worketh righteousness, and speaketh the truth in his heart."*

Action Step

Stay mindful in living a presence-driven life, striving for discernment so that your thoughts and emotions remain anchored in Him. Practice taking captive imaginations and feelings that are rogue in nature, trying to disrupt the peace in your soul. Focus on the root of things rather than the symptoms of a problem. If you are in an intense situation, try to find stillness so that the imagination stands down, and steward your soul as the psalmist practices below.

- Ask, "Why, O my soul, are you downcast?"
- Quiet your soul (see Psalm 131:2).
- Ascribe to the Lord glory and strength (see Psalm 96:6-10).
- Let your soul thirst for God (see Psalm 63:1-2).
- Feel God draw near to your soul (see Psalm 69:18).
- Let God gladden your soul (see Psalm 86:4).
- Hold your soul still, waiting for God (see Psalm 62:1-2).

Prayer

Lord, give me the grace today to remain steady. Let my imaginations not run away within me, and let no trial or circumstance unsettle my soul. Help me continue to experience Your presence today so that I know that I am Your child. I claim my heritage as Your rightful child today.

Journal

Record today's time with the Lord and how He drew you to Him throughout the day. What does it mean to claim your heritage as His rightful child?

Living with Heaven's Glory Mindset

Step 22 / Day 22

Detachment

To detach from the intensity of the world and its head-spinning confusion, we are learning to attach more to the Kingdom. We must learn to detach from here because we are not of this world. Within the first week of my return from Heaven, the Lord showed me how to do this.

He showed me two cities that represent two real-time choices daily. I saw the city on my left, which is everything I don't want to be, everything God gave to man but he corrupted. It's not what it should be. It's a chasing-after-the-wind universe—a modern-day Sodom deeply scarred with hedonism, corruption, and unrighteousness. It's a morning vapor—here today, gone tomorrow.

The city on the right is everything I want to be—the way I know it should be, the way it will be. Where small things are great and everything is pleasing to the eye, lovely, and righteous. This is my Father's world, Yeshua's universe. It's where a lost soul is at the corner waiting to be saved, or one is waiting for prayer. Nothing has changed for 2,000 years in these two contrasting cities or universes.

The first city is the same as it was in Jesus's day. There was political turmoil; there was great poverty and financial difficulty. Most of that society, except for a small group, toiled to make a basic living. There was violence, savagery, and inhumanity, and an unrelenting rule of Rome. Capital punishment by crucifixion was the most painful of deaths. Crime was rampant due to the extraordinary wealth disparity, just like our current time.

To make matters worse, Yeshua was surrounded by paganism and polytheism. Pagan temples dedicated to gods dotted the landscape of the Judean Hellenic world of Yeshua. Roman society was filled with sexual exploits, immorality, perversions. There was governmental corruption on the local and federal level; within Judaism and the temple leadership there was acute corruption (see Matthew 21:12-13). It was in this environment that Yeshua trained His disciples.

He taught them not to overthrow the government. He said to Pilate, *"My kingdom is not of this world. If it were, my servants would fight to prevent my arrest by the Jewish leaders. But now my kingdom is from another place"* (John 18:36 NIV). He taught them how to change man from the inside out through the power of love, telling them that they were in this world but not of it. Then, in the ultimate command on detachment:

> *Everyone who has left houses or brothers or sisters or father or mother or wife or children or fields for my sake will receive a hundred times as much and will inherit eternal life* (Matthew 19:29 NIV).

He instructed the disciples in Matthew 10:14 (AMP), *"Whoever does not welcome you, nor listen to your message, as you leave that house or city, shake the dust [of it] off your feet [in contempt, breaking all ties]."* He taught that people must believe that He would come again and establish God's government.

Also, the requirements to enter the Kingdom of God were repentance, humility, and surrender, not demonstration, violence, and force (see Mark 1:14-15; Matthew 11:12). Yeshua said that we are to set our affections on things above, not on things on the earth (see Philippians 3:16-20).

GLORY LIVING

Since my return, living now a revival life, I set about each morning fixing my back to that city on the left. I detach. Each day I'm looking for a fresh challenge, and for a new soul.

As the first week led into another, I was dancing past the darkness; one year led into the second, and I was no longer letting impermanent things into my soul. My soul was submerged in permanence.

Can you see how these steps can rocket you to a new elevation?

With simple adjustments like these, over time you'll find newly issued spiritual shoes that don't wear out. Each day, you're weaving extraordinary steps, learning, shifting, adjusting, choosing what is better, preferring to see better over worse, goodness over meanness. And the most beautiful accomplishment is being close to everything and not letting it affect you. That's strength! Try it today!

C. S. Lewis said that a continual obsession with looking forward to the eternal world was something that Christians were supposed to do. He wrote in *Mere Christianity,* "It is since Christians have largely ceased to think of the other world that they have become so ineffective in this." He offered this insightful challenge: "Aim at heaven you'll get the earth thrown in:

aim at earth and you'll get neither." Lewis is describing the art of detachment. To get heavenly, one must detach.

Consider the following recommendations:

1. **Do a soul cleanse.** All efforts to begin dancing past the darkness would be intensified if you combined them with *Heaven's Soul Cleanse* (see the back of this book). It will put you in a new operating system and reboot your soul into Heaven-mindedness. When the soul cleanse is completed, detachment is more easily accomplished.

2. **Let the Kingdom consume you.** Practice the tale of two cities—give the world your cold shoulder and gift the lost your attention and heart. Choose to detach from the impermanence of things; identify what you have no control over. Practice Heaven-mindedness.

3. **Be wide-eyed.** Notice the beauty of God's handiwork around you. See God through everything instead of the unsaved, who see God in nothing. We have another universe that compels us.

4. **Focus on the moment.** Look for daily opportunities to share God's love. Watch what God does.

5. **You can't control everything.** You have no power over most things, so let it go and don't miss the simple things.

Journal

Step 23 / Day 23

HUMILITY: THE GREAT PHYSICIAN

NOW LET'S LOOK AT OURSELVES IN THE MIRROR IN THE CONtext of our sinless Savior. As we discover our responsibility in situations, let's begin forgiving and overlooking the weaknesses of others the same way we overlook our own mistakes. This requires a dose of humility! Is that so bad? Could you move that mountain of pride away today and forgive someone who hurt you deeply? You'll never regret it.

The Greek word for humble speaks of our mindset "not rising far from the ground." Its opposite is pride, which means being lifted and rising high above the ground. Humility isn't making yourself look bad or good. Humility is not about making yourself look any way. Actually, humility is the absence of self. Psalm 103:14 (NKJV) states, *"[God] knows our frame; He remembers that we are dust."* We're here for a while, then we disappear.

A familiar saying speaks to our topic: "Be humble enough to see the bigger picture." Perhaps that problematic person in your life serves a developmental purpose. What message is God sending you by putting this person in your life? What reaction does it evoke? Consider the following.

You're a Pearl in the Making: Lessons from the Oyster

Within the oyster, a tiny grain of sand is implanted to stimulate the oyster's immune system. Attempting to rid itself of the irritation, it begins to coat it with a liquid called nacre. Layer by layer it gets larger and more beautiful until it becomes a beautiful pearl.

Similarly, God allows many grains of sand into our lives to irritate us. Why? To become pearl-like in character. You see, He is the great equalizer. That situation in your life is the process by which God is shaping and molding you, performing that beautiful work in you—equalizing the pains and struggles, with the result that finally you have become a gem in His hand.

All too often we seem to not hear the voice of the Lord in the midst of trials. I get it! We're in the middle of a trial, feeling pressed against the situation, and the consternation in our hearts leads to hopelessness. Many who lost family members from COVID know well the despondency they felt. I've seen it in my own family.

But generally, don't immediately blame the other person or situation. Resist and don't respond in kind. Maintain your grip on your position, have self-control, and take the high ground.

Here are some things that you can do. If you are facing a trying circumstance with someone, you are not responsible for their reactions and/or actions but only for your own. Here are some examples.

1. **Say something:** It doesn't require a lengthy letter or a meticulously planned speech when asking for forgiveness. Sometimes a simple gesture of intent, or a word in season, will ignite a tiny spark that brings enough light to penetrate the darkness of a broken relationship. Start by saying, "I'm sorry," "Let's start over," or even, "I'd like to talk." Open doors to start to bring forth healing on both sides.

2. **Break the cycle:** Since we can easily slip into patterns of avoidance in relationships where strife is present, even if you're right, decide to let love and forbearance take over. Have the courage to put blame aside and say, "Let's start over."

3. **Forgive life and people:** Let the past be the past. Sometimes we resent others for the difficult circumstances in our own lives. It's easier to blame other people than to face our disappointments. We need to go one step further. Forgive God for all our frustrations and challenges. Forgive Him when we feel He has hidden His face or when we feel abandoned in our loneliest moments. Forgive Him for the times when it seemed like He gave up on us altogether. Only then can we turn around and say "I'm sorry" to another person.

4. **Ponder Scripture:**

A soft answer turneth away wrath: but grievous words stir up anger (Proverbs 15:1 KJV).

Seest thou a man that is hasty in his words? there is more hope of a fool than of him (Proverbs 29:20 KJV).

Be not rash with thy mouth, and let not thine heart be hasty to utter anything before God; for God is in heaven, and thou upon earth: therefore let thy words be few (Ecclesiastes 5:2 KJV).

Note: Learn more about my life and death in *A Rabbi's Journey to Heaven*.

JOURNAL

Living with Heaven's Glory Mindset

Step 24 / Day 24

HAVING A GLORY PERSPECTIVE

MORE ACUTELY THAN EVER, I CONSIDER THAT TO LEAVE this world is to be with Messiah in His glory, and to remain is to be with Him also in His glory.

Sometimes they are merging. Other times the differences between the world and Heaven are so striking. Often I stop somewhere as I find myself squinting against the fire that surrounded the throne. Heaven was something that I could have only imagined before. Now, and what I have permanently fixed in my spirit and soul, didn't come close to the actual visitation.

Heaven was boundless, borderless, a glorious open habitation of God's magnificence. Uncontested. Untainted. Permanently beautiful. Timeless. Untouched by human hands. Nothing could kiss our soul like Heaven; it was the rarest of rare perfumes, something sweeter than the sweetest taste of a honeycomb.

The waters in Heaven flow and refresh the spirit—not physically, but spiritually. They are running recurrently because they are alive. Fresh. Vibrant. It flows in a perfect, undisturbed rhythm, crawling almost motionlessly forward, but endlessly looping back to where it began—the throne. Everything originates from the throne and around the throne.

Now It's Your Turn

Now I invite you to recall your own grand moments of faith. You have them. That is what I want for you today. Write them down in the journal portion of the devotional. They don't need to be grand like Paul on the road to Damascus or go to the third heaven as he did (see 2 Corinthians 12). Every experience is grand. It's your own unique experience from an all-loving God.

Perhaps it was when you first came to the saving knowledge of Yeshua, or when you were filled with the Holy Spirit. Maybe there was a time when you burst forth in a heavenly language, a miracle, a visitation, a manifestation, a holy epiphany, a theophany, a *rhema* word from God, a divine appointment. Welcome to the adventure and the glory perspective. Pause to remember. Let those memories make their way inside. Within a throng of thoughts perhaps, recall them. Relive them. It will prepare the way forward.

As believers, we cannot conform to the world. Romans 12:2 (NIV) says, *"Do not conform to the pattern of this world, but be transformed by the renewing of your mind. Then you will be able to test and approve what God's will is—his good, pleasing and perfect will."* We choose what is better for the glory mindset, such as peaceful living, solitude, and helping our soul stand down to allow a more glory-centered mindset to take over.

Maintaining a glory perspective takes effort and mindfulness. If you have a holy desire, jump out of life's busyness like a skydiver jumping out of a plane; rediscover memories, answers to prayer, a miracle, and a provision. Today, you need to renew your strength. Mark 6:31 (NIV) says, *"Because so many people were coming and going that they did not even have a chance to eat, he said to [His disciples], 'Come with me by yourselves to a quiet place and get some rest.'"*

As Jesus and his disciples were on their way, he came to a village where a woman named Martha opened her home to him. She had a sister called Mary, who sat at the Lord's feet listening to what he said. But Martha was distracted by all the preparations that had to be made. She came to him and asked, "Lord, don't you care that my sister has left me to do the work by myself? Tell her to help me!" (Luke 10:38-40 NIV).

Listen to these timeless words from our Lord:

"Martha, Martha," the Lord answered, "you are worried and upset about many things, but few things are needed—or indeed only one. Mary has chosen what is better, and it will not be taken away from her" (Luke 10:41-42 NIV).

Choose what is better!

ACTION STEP

Look up and around everywhere. Notice the scurrying around of everyone. Notice how most are caught in the snare of the bustle of the marketplace and its heart-pounding pressure. See His glory. Discover a new understanding when you feel His touch in a loving kiss of faithfulness, a subtle voice in your conscience that brings that peace that surpasses understanding and transcends the murmuring of others (see Philippians 4:7). It's the glory perspective!

Prayer

Lord, open my eyes to Your glory to see the light dwelling in the darkness. Let me not be consumed with the earthly realm today, but only look at my Father's world where a lost soul is waiting on the corner or an individual needs prayer. Your love sustains me daily, and Your hope is still only hoping. Slow me down to see the world around me through Your eyes.

Journal

Record how you saw your day through a glory perspective and not through the carnal realm, i.e., news media, daily reports, etc. Did you find what it means to be in the world and not of it?

> *The Mighty One, God, the Lord, has spoken and summoned the earth, from the rising of the sun to its setting. Out of Zion, the perfection of beauty, God has shone. May our God come and not keep silent; fire devours before Him, and a storm is violently raging around Him. He summons the heavens above, and the earth, to judge His people: "Gather My godly ones to Me, those who have made a covenant with Me by sacrifice." And the heavens declare His righteousness, for God Himself is judge* (Psalm 50:1-6 NASB).

Having a Glory Perspective

Step 25 / Day 25

CROWNS: WHICH DO YOU WANT?

THINK OF THE WONDER IN WHAT GOD HAS APPOINTED for you and me. Every believer who accepts Yeshua is set aside for riches, honor, and an inheritance so great that the mind cannot conceive or think. The untold riches of the world pale in comparison. This morning, let us look at the crowns of the redeemed that will be handed out in heavenly glory.

> *With me are riches and honor, enduring wealth and prosperity. My fruit is better than fine gold; what I yield surpasses choice silver. I walk in the way of righteousness, along the paths of justice, bestowing a rich inheritance on those who love me and making their treasuries full* (Proverbs 8:18-21 NIV).

> *One of the seven angels who had the seven bowls full of the seven last plagues came and said to me, "Come, I will show you the bride, the wife of the Lamb." And he carried me away in the Spirit to a mountain great and high, and showed me the Holy City, Jerusalem, coming down out of heaven from God. It shone with the glory of God, and its brilliance was like that of a very precious jewel, like a jasper, clear as crystal. It had a great, high wall with*

twelve gates, and with twelve angels at the gates. On the gates were written the names of the twelve tribes of Israel (Revelation 21:9-12 NIV).

1. The Crown of Endurance

Do you not know that in a race all the runners run, but only one gets the prize? Run in such a way as to get the prize. Everyone who competes in the games goes into strict training. They do it to get a crown that will not last, but we do it to get a crown that will last forever. Therefore I do not run like someone running aimlessly; I do not fight like a boxer beating the air. No, I strike a blow to my body and make it my slave so that after I have preached to others, I myself will not be disqualified for the prize (1 Corinthians 9:24-27 NIV).

A crown of endurance awaits us for running the race! Stay the course. Remain strong. Don't be fainthearted, but endure and run further in the name of your God than you have ever thought possible. Under all conditions that may come to us, though we may feel fatigued, faintly ashamed at our faults, drained from life, jerked at times back and forth, we are meticulously measured in our Father's hands; everything must be sifted through His fingers.

As long as we sought the service to our Lord in our life, the warmth of His love will be like a sweet vapor rising from the place we find ourselves. Persevere. Push on. Press through.

2. Shepherd's Crown: The Crown of Glory!

To the elders among you, I appeal as a fellow elder and a witness of Christ's sufferings who also will share in the glory to be revealed: Be shepherds of God's flock that is under your care, watching over them—not because you must, but because you are willing, as God wants you to be; not pursuing dishonest gain, but eager to serve; not lording it over those entrusted to you, but being examples to the flock. And when the Chief Shepherd appears, you will receive the crown of glory that will never fade away (1 Peter 5:1-4 NIV).

Perhaps you're a pastor overseeing the sheep. God says, "Remain in Me; your resilience will carry you over the victory line. Let no fatigue, disappointment, or struggle overtake you. Be not caught off guard, but search for My hiding place, the cleft of the rock that I have reserved for you." Be concealed in my shadow, says the Lord.

The shepherd's crown is to restore the soul of many. He brings the lost soul home and soothes the wounds of those hurt through life's hardships. He embraces them with a tender arm and allows his words to be a soothing balm on a parched soul. He helps them repent by helping them to understand what sin they have committed. Repentance through knowledge ensures that a soul stays fixed in the redemption of our Lord.

What a privilege to be called a shepherd.

3. Sufferer's Crown

Blessed is the man who remains steadfast under trial, for when he has stood the test he will receive the crown of life, which God has promised to those who love him (James 1:12 ESV).

This crown is for bearing up under trial! The sufferer's crown! Blessed is the one who perseveres under trial because when they have stood the test, they will receive the crown of life God promised to those who love Him.

There is much suffering in the world today. Nerves can be knitted into a tangled mess of confusion, disappointment, and fear. Everything can feel wrong, and more is wrong today than right. But God says, "Push your shoulders back and stride forward in a newfound faith and assurance in Me." Our Messiah, our High Priest, is advocating for you today, seeking you, reaching down to you, lifting you, reestablishing you, anointing you, carrying you to a new place of His presence.

4. Crown of Faithfulness

Do not be afraid of what you are about to suffer. I tell you, the devil will put some of you in prison to test you, and you will suffer persecution for ten days. Be faithful, even to the point of death, and I will give you life as your victor's crown (Revelation 2:10 NIV).

- By faith Abel brought God a better offering than Cain did. By faith he was commended as righteous when God spoke well of his offerings.

And by faith Abel still speaks, even though he is dead.

- By faith Enoch was taken from this life so that he did not experience death: "He could not be found, because God had taken him away." For before he was taken, he was commended as one who pleased God. And without faith it is impossible to please God, because anyone who comes to Him must believe that He exists and that He rewards those who earnestly seek Him.

- By faith Noah, when warned about things not yet seen, in holy fear built an ark to save his family. By his faith he condemned the world and became heir of the righteousness that is in keeping with faith.

- By faith Abraham, when God tested him, offered Isaac as a sacrifice. He who had embraced the promises was about to sacrifice his one and only son, even though God had said to him, "It is through Isaac that your offspring will be reckoned." Abraham reasoned that God could even raise the dead, and so in a manner of speaking he did receive Isaac back from death.

These were all commended for their faith, yet none of them received what had been promised, since God had planned something better for them so that only together with us would they be made perfect (see Hebrews 11:4,5-6,7,17-19,39-40 NIV). What will your faith look like when the Lord returns to fulfill His promise?

5. Crown of Righteousness

Now there is in store for me the crown of righteousness, which the Lord, the righteous Judge, will award to me on that day—and not only to me, but also to all who have longed for his appearing (2 Timothy 4:8 NIV).

Action Step

Meditate on the five crowns of glory that await us. Consider how your life matches up with the life of each crown. How can you realign your life with them? Are you still running the race, bearing up under suffering and pressure? Are you enduring in faithfulness? Today is a day of reflection.

Prayer

Lord, help me be stronger during suffering and trial today. Give me the strength to run the race of glory for You and live each day in the light of Your glory, presence, and power.

Journal

Record in your journal your reflections on your life, considering the five crowns.

Living with Heaven's Glory Mindset

Step 26 / Day 26

Having Self-Control

But the fruit of the Spirit is love, joy, peace, forbearance, kindness, goodness, faithfulness, gentleness and self-control. Against such things there is no law (Galatians 5:22-23 NIV).

Sometimes we find ourselves in situations and relationships that we regret. We open doors to conversations that we shouldn't. Sometimes we press for information that we regret hearing. Sometimes we must swallow down the hurt that roars inside us and wish we could scream from the mountaintops the pain and injustice, but we can't. So we bite our lips in frustration. Our forehead wrinkles in pain and frustration, and the irrelevant whys of the thing stop us. Or there's an inherent indignity in it all. It's all true!

Self-control (see Galatians 5:22-23) is not only a fruit of the spirit but an art learned that steers the ship away from many disasters.

Self-control, or temperance, is moderation in action, thought, or feeling, and the ability to control ourselves. One of the defining signs of God working in us is having control of our thoughts, words, and actions. Our fallen nature is the contrarian trying to waylay us to lose control. Lack of self-control is like a team of wild horses breaking free from their restraints.

Now all of us have seen the consequences of what happens when self-control is absent. Relationships, ministries, marriages, and souls have all been destroyed from a lack of self-control. Reactiveness and impulse can fill up a cemetery with its victims.

> *Better a patient person than a warrior, one with self-control than one who takes a city* (Proverbs 16:32 NIV).
>
> *For this very reason, make every effort to add to your faith goodness; and to goodness, knowledge; and to knowledge, self-control; and to self-control, perseverance; and to perseverance, godliness; and to godliness, mutual affection; and to mutual affection, love* (2 Peter 1:5-7 NIV).
>
> *The tongue has the power of life and death, and those who love it will eat its fruit* (Proverbs 18:21 NIV).
>
> *My dear brothers and sisters, take note of this: Everyone should be quick to listen, slow to speak and slow to become angry* (James 1:19 NIV).

Lesson: Don't let things interrupt your peace and steadiness. Strive to have feet of iron that remain firm in His presence today. Sometimes we must bite our lower lip even if the other person is right. Promise the Lord today that you will not reply in kind to anybody or anything that comes your way but strive to stay in a holy intention to control your soul. Let the single extent of security in Messiah arise from His love for you.

During a day, we can be shocked by someone's questions, actions, and remarks. Sometimes we respond automatically, uncensored, out of guilt, anger, or hurt. We sometimes want to change the subject because we cannot honestly hold steady without being on the verge of an explosion. Let the single measure of comfort come from His love for you.

Action Step

Today, be resolved to be steadfast in your emotions, to not lose control of your thoughts, words, and actions. When something happens today, practice self-control and the vital fruit of the Holy Spirit. Galatians 5:22-23 tells us the Spirit produces love, joy, peace, patience, kindness, goodness, faithfulness, humility, and self-control.

Prayer

Lord, give me the strength to be strong, my heart steady, my words carefully chosen. Hold tightly today, Lord, that I would have self-control throughout my day, learning to be steadily secured through the tempests and trials.

Journal

Enter into your journal what God revealed today to be firm and robust amid temptation and the pressures of the day. Give two testimonies of situations when you didn't respond in kind, and thank the Lord for His strength.

Better a patient person than a warrior, one with self-control than one who takes a city (Proverbs 16:32 NIV).

The tongue has the power of life and death, and those who love it will eat its fruit (Proverbs 18:21 NIV).

Fools occasionally show their annoyance at once, but the prudent overlook an insult (Proverbs 12:16 NIV).

Unto You I lift up my eyes, O You who are enthroned in the heavens! Behold, as the eyes of servants look to the hand of their master, and as the eyes of a maid to the hand of her mistress, so our eyes look to the Lord our God, until He is gracious and favorable toward us (Psalm 123:1-2 AMP).

Having Self-Control

Step 27 / Day 27

A True Disciple

To be a true disciple, it starts with learning to please our Lord and ends with pleasing our Lord. In the middle are the lines and lines of white, not gray or black. We are staying within these lines until we are close enough to see our Father's eyes when we get to glory. It always begins with one little step chosen from the eternities of time—we give our lives to the Lord and are born again to become disciples. Every day of every year, it's the same. It always begins with one little step.

Knowing what pleases our Lord is essential. Luke 10:21 (NIV) says,

At that time Jesus, full of joy through the Holy Spirit, said, "I praise you, Father, Lord of heaven and earth, because you have hidden these things from the wise and learned, and revealed them to little children."

Yeshua was "full of joy." He seemed to jump for joy and was exceedingly glad. In Luke 10:17, we learn that the 72 recruits returned with joy and said, *"Lord, even the demons submit to us in Your name."* At that moment, the 72 became His disciples because they obeyed and followed the instructions of their Master. A true disciple will continue in His work, which Yeshua expects from us. We have denied true discipleship if we serve only when convenient or easy. Let's look at three disciples. All three stood by, watching our Lord closely.

THE FIRST DISCIPLE

As they were walking along the road, a man said to him, "I will follow you wherever you go." Jesus replied, "Foxes have dens and birds have nests, but the Son of Man has no place to lay his head" (Luke 9:57-58 NIV).

There was no counting the cost in the first prospective disciple. Hastiness marked this one! He thought that in his strength, he could do it. After all, Yeshua had given up the entire world that He knew in the glories of Heaven. This disciple seemed to stand in his self-reliance and enthusiasm, but weakness was present. When it began to cost something or got complex, his enthusiasm quickly waned. Observe the Lord's response—He accepted the offer but sent the man to prayer and self-review in one swift statement of truth.

Yeshua stated in Luke 9:58 that He didn't even own a place to lay His head: *"Foxes have dens to live in, and birds have nests, but I, the Messiah, have no earthly home at all."* He was saying, "Don't you know I am the poorest? Don't you know I am the one rejected and despised? No throne, no royalty, no kingdom as you perceive." Our Lord did not trust his too-ready enthusiasm. He knew it would not stand the test of time—or the self-sacrifice that always comes with greater responsibility.

Conclusion: The first seeker was impulsive, even thoughtless in his enthusiasm—one who would begin without counting the cost. This made him more suited to the life of a country squire than to join in ruling in the kingdom on earth.

THE SECOND DISCIPLE

He said to another man, "Follow me." But he replied, "Lord, first let me go and bury my father." Jesus said to him, "Let the dead bury their own dead, but you go and proclaim the kingdom of God" (Luke 9:59-60 NIV).

At another time, Yeshua invited a man to come with Him and be His disciple. The man agreed but wanted to wait until his father's death. He was the only one of the three who received a divine call! He said, "Lord, first let me go and bury my father." In the first disciple, the initiative was taken by the man. Here, the initiative was taken by Messiah. His father had not yet died, and the man felt obligated to care for him until he died. The Lord looked into the heart of this man and saw the conflict—too much gold mingled with the worries and concerns of the earth! The Lord's answer was a resounding no. The Lord's call often sets private and domestic demands aside. The man didn't correct himself either but disappeared from the scene and was never heard from again.

We are tempted to think that our duty to our relations will excuse us from our commitment to Christ. If our nearest and dearest stand in our way and keep us from Messiah, it will be necessary to have a zeal to make us forget father and mother. Many are tempted to rest in discipleship and remain a loose end, never giving of themselves to be strict and constant in the service of the Kingdom of our Lord.

THE THIRD DISCIPLE

Still another said, "I will follow you, Lord; but first let me go back and say goodbye to my family." Jesus replied, "No one who puts a hand to the plow and looks back is fit for service in the kingdom of God" (Luke 9:61-62 NIV).

This is the tender-hearted disciple. He said, "I will follow You, Lord, but first let me go back and say goodbye to my family." Jesus replied, "No one who puts a hand to the plow and looks back is fit for service in the kingdom of God." With this man, there was very little hope of any real work to be done throughout his life. That is why Yeshua was hard on him. I would feel a dull pang watching him walk away. He was the perfect audience, ready to be welcomed into the service of the King. But he looked just like the others, and so many who face the same experiences walk away as he did.

On the rocks and reefs of the sea, we find plant life so deeply rooted that they are almost impossible to remove. Yet the only changes that occur are by the natural ebb and flow of the current. Many people of God are like these plants—they are so rooted in the concerns of this life. The only change and variety come from life's natural ebb and flow. Day after day, their life is dictated by earthly events—a soul cleaving to the soil of this world.

Perhaps you were once one of them and a genuine player in this timeless drama. Let me say that the music is starting again, and the procession is lining up for you to follow again in God's call upon your life. No more clenching fists because you have every right to be here now.

Conclusion: All three said noble, honorable things, yet all three were not used! Yeshua knew the hearts of these people.

- First, he could not understand there was a cost—he was impulsive and fleshly.
- Second, though he was divinely called, he was too consumed with the ties of this world.
- Third, his heart was filled with soulish relationships that robbed him of the *kairos* moment upon him.

Prayer

Lord, help me to be Your disciple. Please give me the willingness and courage to follow You in this day faithfully, and let no earthly relationship block the way You have for me. I ask, Lord, that You forgive me for any double-mindedness and strengthen me to be Your disciple.

Journal

A True Disciple

Step 28 / Day 28

Morning Jump Exercise

Morning jump exercise. Today is about jumping out of the earthly realm and into the spiritual world of our great God. Saturate your soul today with these jump exercises.

Now your forehead is likely wrinkled, and you are wondering how you can do that. Well, get ready!

Begin to recall the power of God and His love in your life—the memories of God's faithfulness, healing, grace, your former passion, and times you witnessed to a lost soul coming to faith, perhaps when praying for someone to be healed. We're drawing water up here from a deep well, your most profound memories of a great God. You're jumping out of the carnal mind and into the spirit.

Since we are made body, soul, and spirit, your soul needs to be fed. *"Come and hear, all you who fear God, and I will tell what he has done for my soul"* (Psalm 66:16 ESV). You can do this while driving, sitting, working, or anywhere. Such emotions are latent impulses every child of God has been imprinted with.

If you need some inspiration, visualize the pillar of fire that descended from Heaven to rest in the night sky, and the cloud by day that accompanied God's ancient people in their wanderings.

Morning Jump Exercise

Reflect on the fire on the altar on Mount Moriah as Abraham brought Isaac to be sacrificed. Can you visualize the fire red hot and ready, flickering and dancing, blinking, popping as it sends sparks into the air? Abraham, perhaps dumbstruck, holding a large knife in his hand that will work its way into his son's throat soon—his only son, Isaac. What is in his mind? One can only imagine. Every second hangs heavy, looming large with suspense. I can see Abraham's pulse like a machine gun firing inside his chest.

Then move your mind's eye over to the Red Sea, seeing it split in two as two walls of water stood up to make a dry path for the Israelites to pass through. I see every Israelite moving with a steadying hand on the back of the other, carefully, quietly, children fearfully staying in step, following one another one by one, pushing, hurrying. Perhaps whispering over the shoulder of the next, "Stay steady; look forward. Pharaoh's mighty army is on our heels."

I see the last Israelites place their feet on the other side, and there is a momentary pause. Everyone hears a strange roar; it's the sea folding back. They turn to look, only to observe the sea opening its mouth like a giant Leviathan swallowing up Pharaoh's mighty army. I see Pharaoh sitting on the other side in utter shock. Wiped off the face of the earth are his army, firstborn son, and empire.

In another scene, I admit my dismay. When I visualize the death of my Messiah—I don't want to see it. Then jubilation sweeps over me at the empty tomb—followed by thoughts of Pentecost in the Upper Room.

There is an important point here that I want to introduce you to. Our entire life is like a stone vault filled with heavenly meditations and memories. They may not be as grand as the ones mentioned, but yours fit you. Yours are as extraordinary and miraculous. They are like your personal arrows in your quiver that you can shoot into the night sky, releasing fireworks of reflections of His greatness and faithfulness in your life. Go ahead, enter your vault, sit for a moment, and shoot your arrows into the night. Recall your memories. There are too many glories to count. Choose which one.

Action Step

During your morning devotional time, begin to visualize the greatness of God even right now, and start to rehearse it in your mind. Indeed, you can thank the Lord for things in your life despite those trials and disappointments. Open that concrete vault and free your thoughts and imaginations of His majesty, power, and love! Let your thoughts be upon the miracles He has performed, and declare His blessings for your life today and tomorrow. Jump out of the temporal realm and into the spiritual realm to see it!

Prayer

Father, thank You for Your miracle-working power—that You, Lord, are the same yesterday, today, and tomorrow. Thank You for all Your benefits and Your love in my life—Your faithfulness from one generation to the next. Help me share Your love with someone today and pray for a miracle in their life. Let the Kingdom in me operate entirely today!

JOURNAL

Make a list of the miracles God has done in your life—your experiences with the supernatural operation of His presence. List them so you can call them to memory. Record an interaction with someone today who needed a miracle and you were able to pray for them.

Living with Heaven's Glory Mindset

Step 29 / Day 29

SETTING YOUR SPIRITUAL TEMPERATURE

Prayer, meditation, and solitude are essential life principles for the child of God. We need them as our bodies need food and water.

When the Lord revealed how I was to pray following my return from Heaven, I saw the difference between transactional prayer and the transformational model, a more heavenly pattern. The Lord said that in my silence and prayer time, I was not to let desire and want taint my time with Him, for they would only distract me from living in the present within the presence. This became the cradle of transformational prayer, and I began to experience a profound transformation. I understood the following:

- Let no vague impressions of my past and shadowy images of my future lead me astray from what is.
- Let not my silence be filled with thought, for thoughts are only fleeting ideas and concepts surveyed by the mind and measured by human understanding.

- Instead, let my silence be confined by time and space but open to infinity that embraces all possibilities and the mystery of eternity in every moment within—all that is.
- Let not my silence be disturbed by views of duality in which a division between Him and me is perceived as truth, separating the experience of what is from the expression of self. But let the I AM and thou merge into the silence of conscious awareness that exists in the eternal now where we may dwell in the oneness of God with whom we live and move and have our being.

Part of this process is changing your prayer life to 75 percent exaltation and magnification of the great I AM. Imagine when 75 percent of your time glorifies your heavenly Father and 25 percent asks Him for stuff. This is not how we were taught, and I imagine you nodding and agreeing. But this my friend, is the purpose of the 30 days in His glory in *Heaven's Soul Cleanse* and *A Rabbi's Journey to Heaven*.

You're Ready!

The morning is here, and you are ready for your adventure. In the morning, all is calm and quiet, so strive to get up early before the sounds of life begin. When your surroundings are peaceful, it is easier for your mind and soul to follow, and a good time for the Lord to speak. Here is what the Bible reveals about the mornings:

> *Let me hear in the morning of your steadfast love, for in you I trust. Make me know the way I should go, for to you I lift up my soul* (Psalm 143:8 ESV).
>
> *I will sing of your strength; I will sing aloud of your steadfast love in the morning. For you have been to me a fortress and a refuge in the day of my distress* (Psalm 59:16 ESV).
>
> *But I, O Lord, cry to you; in the morning my prayer comes before you* (Psalm 88:13 ESV).
>
> *Satisfy us in the morning with your steadfast love, that we may rejoice and be glad all our days* (Psalm 90:14 ESV).
>
> *I rise before dawn and cry for help; I hope in your words* (Psalm 119:147 ESV).

During this time, resist the urge to ask God for something. Stop! Catch yourself and start again. In the beginning, it will feel awkward. During this time, refrain from petitioning, praising, or giving thanks. This is a time of complete exaltation, adoration, and enlargement of our heavenly Father. Review the following:

1. **Praise is "I" centered.** We are constantly thanking Him for what He has done for "me" and "us." This is not the time for that.
2. **Petition is "I" centered.** "Lord, please help me, deliver me, and alleviate my situation." Again, this is not the time for that.
3. **Glory psalms are God centered.** "Lord, You are glorious and majestic in all Your ways." "You set the stars in place and call them by name."

"From day unto day, and night unto night, You are there." "From eternities past to the eternities that await Your creation, You shall always be upon Your glorious throne." "Nothing compares to Your greatness."

4. **Begin at the same time every morning.** Whatever time you are accustomed to spending with God, end it for the day. Do no further reading for the day. Allow the Word to wash over you.

5. **After three days or so, you will begin to sense a different perception of your day.** God, the Creator, will start to permeate your mind. You will be more perceptive of His handprint everywhere.

Example

You, oh Lord, are the Maker of Heaven and earth, the Steward of life, the Creator and Sustainer. Without You, there would be nothing. Without You, the world would be dark and lifeless. You, Father, are perfect and holy, forgiving, compassionate. Always, Lord, You are slow to anger and quick to forgive.

Who is like You among the gods? There are no works like Yours. You are great and do beautiful things. You alone are God. As You are a statute for Israel, a rule for the God of Jacob, You have decreed our lives for eternity. You gave us Your Son, the steadfast and Holy One. Without Him, we would be lost in a deep forest of despair. Without Him, we would be swept away like a piece of wood carried away by the ocean. You, Lord, have become our hope; only You are the utmost Holy

One. Is there anything more significant? No! Is there anyone more important? No!

An important note: Transformation or elevation prayers are absent of I, me, us, my, mine, or we. Whom do you see? Your Father. Wow! Get ready to swim in the river of God! Remember, it's about healing your soul and entering a higher plane of peaceful living.

Action Step

Today, we practice loving God. No petition, praise or thanksgiving, but only exaltation and magnification. Tell Him how wonderfully gracious and loving He is. Meditate on the readings offered in this days devotion, and let it marinate in your soul. Give Him you burdens today, and leave them in The Fathers hands.

Your focus is not on yourself, me, mine, our, or us. In this day I want you to simply meditate on Him and all that He created.

Prayer

Father, help me to see those things that I pass by daily. Help me to look up, realizing that YOU are sitting enthroned over my life, Knowing each moment and step of my day. Help me to be a lover of Your presence, and an admirer of Your creation, to find moments of solitude with You. Lord, thank-you for Your Love, Your glory, and the King of Glory that changed my life!

Journal

Write in your journal your experience in the day and how the Lord directed you to someone to minister to.

Step 30 / Day 30

TO THE JEW FIRST

THE APOSTLE PAUL TELLS US, "FOR I AM NOT ASHAMED OF the gospel, for it is the power of God for salvation to everyone who believes, to the Jew first and also to the Greek" (Romans 1:16 ESV). Whatever evangelistic agency resides in us, the process, according to Paul, is to the Jew first.

It used to be that many thought that the Jews were the rejected people of God, and when God had completed His work amongst the Gentiles, the Jews would then become His focus. Of course, these flawed views (replacement theology and dispensationalism)[1] have been enormous stumbling stones to salvation for the Jewish people.

To consider God's eternal plans and purposes, the God of Heaven planned for the gospel to go out from Jerusalem. Yet the plan of redemption is not limited to the Jewish people or Israel. It starts from Jerusalem and will expand to all the world's nations. To the Jew first and then the Greek. This outreach model to the Jew first is not an afterthought but a priority.

The disciples taught us to fulfill God's calling while keeping His priorities straight. Paul always preached to the Jew first. He went into the synagogues first, despite an unwelcoming reception (see Acts 13:14; 14:1; 17:1-2,10,16-17; 18:4,19; 19:8; 28:17). He expertly challenged his Greek audience that loved philosophy (see Acts 17:16-34; 14:15-17). To the Jew, he became a Jew, preaching and teaching according to the ways of his people (see 1 Corinthians 9:20-22). He says that he became all things to all people (see 1 Corinthians 9:20-22).

Paul provides a beautiful picture of the Gentile calling in Romans 11:11 (ESV): *"So I ask, did they stumble in order that they might fall? By no means! Rather, through their trespass salvation has come to the Gentiles, so as to make Israel jealous."* The Gentile is to make the Jew envious of their relationship with the God of Abraham, Isaac, and Jacob and demonstrate the Jewish Messiah's love. Then in verse 12 (ESV), the cause of celebration is introduced: *"Now if their trespass means riches for the world, and if their failure means riches for the Gentiles, how much more will their full inclusion mean!"*

Suppose we were to now consider the richness of the body when the Jewish people come to faith—we see a completion of the plan of God. In that case, fulfillment can come by bringing Jewish people back into the family of God, to reestablish the Jew in the calling that God placed upon them. This Gentile assignment doesn't need a divine call of God to love the Jew and support Jewish ministry any more than one needs a divine call to share the gospel with lost souls. Such things are implicit and universally tasked to all of us.

How to Apply Romans 1:16

Even though we are different culturally, we are the same; Jew and Gentile are two siblings in the family of God. The Jew is the firstborn (see Exodus 4:22; Jeremiah 31:9); the Gentile is the second born. Both are equally loved and equally called. Prioritize outreach efforts to Jewish people, give to Jewish ministry, and be willing to be trained to witness Yeshua in a Jewish-friendly way.

Action Steps

1. Pray for the peace of Jerusalem (see Psalm 122:6).
2. Share the gospel with Jewish people (see Romans 1:16).
3. Learn how to be a witness of the truth to the Jewish people effectively.
4. Support Jewish ministries that are reaching Jewish people in tithes and offerings.
5. Become a prayer partner to undergird Jewish ministry, interceding for the salvation of the Jewish people.

Prayer

Lord, give me a heart and love for the Jewish people, so that the redeeming work You have done in my life, would be shared with Your firstborn. Help me to be a blessing to Jewish ministries reaching Your people, and help me to be Your ambassador of Romans 1:16.

Journal

Write in your journal your understanding of God's heart for the Jews and your experience sharing the gospel with them. Share your apprehensions, fears, testimonies, and victories.

Living with Heaven's Glory Mindset

NOTE

1. **Replacement theology:** The New Testament church has replaced Israel and has become the new spiritual Israel. The blessings directed to Israel and the Jewish people are transferred to the Gentile Christian church, but the curses remain on the shoulders of the Jewish people. Gentile Christians then become spiritual Jews, and the Jewish people lose their calling and distinction. **Dispensationalism:** God is working specifically among the nations. Only when He is finished and the full number of the Gentiles come in (see Romans 11:25) will God turn His attention to the Jews. Consequently, dispensationalists say there is no need to witness to Jewish people because it is not their time.

Step 31 / Day 31

Honoring Israel and the Jewish People

I will bless those who bless you, and him who dishonors you I will curse, and in you all the families of the earth shall be blessed (Genesis 12:3 ESV).

TODAY'S DEVOTIONAL CELEBRATES THE DISTINCTIONS OF Israel and the Jewish people. We cannot complete this 31-day devotional without it due to God's covenant with them. Here we offer a brief overview of their distinctions.

In Romans, we learn that the Jewish people were given an irrevocable calling and election according to Romans 11:28-29 (CSB): *"Regarding the gospel, they are enemies for your advantage, but regarding election, they are loved because of the patriarchs, since God's gracious gifts and calling are irrevocable."*

Let me say that honoring Israel and the Jewish people will take a church into uncharted waters of blessing—the ultimate consequence of Genesis 12:3 (KJV): *"I will bless them that bless thee, and curse him that curseth thee."* Recognizing the Jewish people who preserved the Bible and brought the gospel to the nations is to seek their good and destiny as a people. Despite historical antisemitism, this viewpoint chooses to attach to the divine foundation of the family of God. Consider the following list of distinctions of Israel:

Distinct Calling

The Jewish people have a distinct calling and history with God. God personally and directly chose no other nation and people. They have a direct covenant with God, communicated through the Abrahamic Covenant, the Land Covenant, the Davidic Covenant (see 2 Samuel 7:10-11), and the New Covenant (see Hebrews 8). God gave no other nation a specific land to call their own that He would return to. Hence, the Jewish people can trace their history and occupation back to a homeland more than 3,000 years old (see Genesis 12).

Distinct History

The Jewish people have a distinct history. No other nation or people has been systematically pursued for destruction. Yet no other country and people rest at the center of an interpersonal relationship with God, that unfolds from one chapter to the next. Israel is called the "wife of Jehovah" in the Old Testament, and the relationship goes through many stages:

- Marriage (see Ezekiel 16:8)
- Adultery (see Jeremiah 3:1-5,20; 31:32; Ezekiel 16:15-34; Hosea 2:2-5)
- Separation (see Isaiah 50:1)
- Divorce (see Jeremiah 3:6-10)
- Punishment (see Ezekiel 16:35-43; Hosea 2:6-13)
- Remarriage with restored blessings (see Jeremiah 31:31-34; Ezekiel 16:60-63; Isaiah 54:1-8; 62:4-5; Hosea 2:14-23)

Distinct Prophetic Destiny

No other people and land have a distinct prophetic destiny. No other nation was given an irrevocable calling with clear, specific details (see Deuteronomy 28:13; 15:6; Hosea 1:11; Romans 11:15). No other nation is essential to the return of the Lord, and the completion of the Messianic order (see Romans 11:29).

Distinct Relationship

No other nation has been called to be a servant and priestly nation to the Gentile nations. God told no other country that all other nations would be blessed if they blessed them and cursed if they cursed them (see Isaiah 42:6; Genesis 12:3; Exodus 19:6).

Distinct Identity

No other nation is called God's firstborn son, the apple of His eye, His chosen people, or peculiar treasure. No other nation was given the covenant of circumcision to make a physical distinction from the nations (see Exodus 4:22; Jeremiah 31:9).

Action Step

Share the love of God with a Jewish person today. If you don't know any, or no Jewish people exist in your life circle or work life, take the time to pray for the salvation of the Jewish people. Pray for the peace of Jerusalem and the salvation of all Israel.

Prayer

Lord, give me boldness to share Your love with the Jewish people (see Romans 1:16). Lord, I pray for the peace of Jerusalem and the salvation of all Israel (see Psalm 122:6). Let the valley of dry bones come alive in this hour and bring the harvest of Jewish souls to Messiah (see Ezekiel 37). Let my life be used for You, Lord, to be a light to Your firstborn.

> *For I am not ashamed of the gospel, because it is the power of God that brings salvation to everyone who believes: first to the Jew, then to the Gentile* (Romans 1:16 NIV).

JOURNAL

Living with Heaven's Glory Mindset

BONUS DAY

Seek First the Kingdom

When life is shaken and foundations are rocked, a man shouts from the mountaintop that his way is the way, his words should be the steps that we walk. Then, in an instant, I am reminded that You, Lord, have become a shelter for the oppressed and no other. You are a refuge in times of trouble and no other. Your name is trustworthy and no other. But seek the Kingdom of God and His righteousness first, and all these things shall be added unto you (see Matthew 6:33).

ONE INWARD EVIDENCE OF SEEKING FIRST THE KINGDOM OF God is simplicity, which involves a life of joyful unconcern for possessions. It has nothing to do with possessions but the control of possessions on an individual. It is an inward celebration of the spirit of trust.

Solomon wrote in Proverbs 14:12 (NKJV), *"There is a way that seems right to a man, but its end is the way of death."* Jeremiah said, *"O Lord, I know the way of man is not in himself; it is not in man who walks to direct his own steps"* (Jeremiah 10:23 NKJV).

Seeking the Kingdom of God and His righteousness, first introduces us to living in service to Him. And this service is not to be our private secret. Selflessness is the quantum, the milestone to reach. Yeshua embodied selflessness. We need to swing away from worrying, to serving.

Yet we are often limited by our pressures, needs, and perceived timing in our life. The exact opposite is true. Selflessness and service are the surest roads to inner peace during the pressures. They lift you. They rise up in the very act of service. We learn to let go of the external and internal pressure, as we displace worry for the high calling.

Not that you haven't noticed, but there is never perfect timing for selflessness or service.

Yeshua's teaching on *"seek first the kingdom of God"* (see Matthew 6:33) is in the context of not worrying about the realities of life, such as food, shelter, clothing, and so forth. It could be seen as one of the most consequential sermons on living successfully in the Kingdom.

> *Therefore I tell you, do not worry about your life, what you will eat or drink; or about your body, what you will wear. Is not life more than food, and the body more than clothes? Look at the birds of the air; they do not sow or reap or store away in barns, and yet your heavenly Father feeds them. Are you not much more valuable than they? Can any one of you by worrying add a single hour to your life?*
>
> *And why do you worry about clothes? See how the flowers of the field grow. They do not labor or spin. Yet I tell you that not even Solomon in all his splendor was dressed like one of these. If that is how God*

clothes the grass of the field, which is here today and tomorrow is thrown into the fire, will he not much more clothe you—you of little of faith? So do not worry, saying, "What shall we eat?" or "What shall we drink?" or "What shall we wear?" For the pagans run after all these things, and your heavenly Father knows that you need them (Matthew 6:25-32 NIV).

We can romanticize seeking first the Kingdom, but we were born to care. Our Master's life led the way as He, the Son of God, washed His disciples' feet and wept in the face of many sufferings. His Spirit was put in us.

Service, and learning empathy, are the antidote to selfishness and consumption. It teaches us to accept others by pulling us out of our silos to encounter different people at all seasons of life—grief, homelessness, bankruptcy, loneliness, etc.

Suddenly, we see our life in a greater context than ourselves, as service counters hate, prejudice, and ignorance. It allows *agape* love to flow. Yeshua demonstrated this kind of divine love to humanity in the way He lived and died:

For God so loved the world that he gave his one and only Son, that whoever believes in him shall not perish but have eternal life (John 3:16 NIV).

I think of one incident that emerged with the believers in Rome over whether Christians should eat meat that might have been previously offered to idols. The apostle Paul had to remind them to step back and look at the bigger picture. He wrote, *"The kingdom of God is not eating and drinking, but righteousness and peace and joy in the Holy Spirit"* (Romans 14:17 NKJV).

The Bible teaches us that God is righteous and just, evenly tempered with abounding mercy, and He calls upon us to emulate Him. *"Ye shall be holy, for I the Lord your God am holy"* (Leviticus 19:2 KJV). God's righteousness and mercy apply to everyone—those who hold to pro-choice or pro-life, a criminal or a law-abiding individual.

One's political ideology does not influence God, nor does He alter His standards for any individual or nation. God is extending His heart of compassion to the sinner and yet always detests the sin. All are God's children, and all have fallen short of the mercy and glory of God.

Action Step

Today, be mindful of the simplicity of the Kingdom that God wants for you. Look to share *agape* love so that you can be a shining light for someone today.

Don't be trapped today in a system counter to the Kingdom of God.

Keep your day simple, have little solitudes throughout the day, and share the love of God with someone.

Filter out any disregard for the homeless in your heart, the oppressed, the poor, the disadvantaged, and the widow. Let prejudice or judgment not shine its face upon you today. Rise with mercy and love.

Prayer

Lord, help me not be worried and consumed with material things, but let me find contentment in my station in the presence of Your life in me. Let me have an attitude of gratitude for all You have given me. Please help me to pursue the Kingdom first in my life.

Journal

Record how you pursued the Kingdom first in your day. What opportunities came to you to choose between the Kingdom of God and the kingdom of the world?

Living with Heaven's Glory Mindset

Seek First the Kingdom

Living with Heaven's Glory Mindset

About Felix Halpern

Felix Halpern was born in 1952 in the Netherlands. As a child, his family immigrated to the United States, where he was raised in northern New Jersey. Before full-time ministry, he established a lucrative career in the precious metals and diamond industries at the International Diamond Center of New York City. Immersed for nearly two decades in the Orthodox and Hasidic Jewish communities, he gave his life to the salvation of the Jewish people.

Coming from a rich Jewish heritage, he is also rooted in Nazi resistance. Rabbi Halpern's paternal grandfather was an Orthodox rabbi and leader of his synagogue in Germany. His maternal grandparents established one of the many underground resistance movements against Hitler throughout the Netherlands. His father received the knowledge and understanding of his Messiah while being hidden with other Jews after miraculously escaping Germany.

Ministry Today

Today, Felix Halpern ministers nationally and internationally with a message of restoration between Jew and Gentile and the anointing of the evangelist. He serves as a nationally appointed missionary to the Jewish people. For twenty years, he and his wife, Bonnie, have served as senior leaders of a Messianic congregation they founded, Beth Chofesh (House of Freedom).

He pioneered the first national Jewish fellowship of the Assemblies of God and served the first four years as its president. He has also served as a general presbyter for the Assemblies of God, on the AG Board of Ethnicity, and the Lost Lamb Evangelistic Association Board.

In 2013 God provided the means to form the first resource office for Jewish ministry within the Assemblies of God in the greater New York and New Jersey metropolitan region, called Metro Jewish Resources.

In 2019, Rabbi Felix suffered a fatal heart attack due to medical malpractice. He experienced the supernatural crossing over as his body was dead, and he experienced the throne of God and life in the third heaven. God gave his life back, and following this he authored *A Rabbi's Journey to Heaven* and *Heaven's Soul Cleanse*, featured by Sid Roth ministries. His life-and-death experience and his journey into the third heaven established Chofesh Ministries (Freedom Ministries) in 2020.

Contact Information

Rabbi Felix Halpern
P.O. Box 3777
Wayne, NJ 07470
email: hisglobalglory@gmail.com
Website: www.Chofesh.org

From
FELIX HALPERN

30 Days of His Glory

It all happened suddenly. In a twinkling of an eye. Rabbi Felix died, left his body, and crossed over into heaven. Amazed, he experienced the glories of heaven that he had only read, pondered, and dreamt about.

In these extraordinary heavenly experiences, Rabbi Felix's eyes were opened to life-changing truths about the spiritual world that he shares with you.

Imagine submerging your soul in the Glory of God, and starving your soul of the natural for 30 days! For 30 days you will drown your soul in the Glory and magnification of God! You will experience heaven's operating system as it was given to Rabbi Felix. You will be launched into a daily living where you have a sky over your life and no longer a ceiling.

Heaven's Soul Cleanse is 100% biblical, and 100% centered upon the magnification and enlargement of God's glory and presence. It is guaranteed to imprint your soul and transform your mind. No longer will you be burdened by mortal pressures; no longer will you ask God repeatedly for the same thing. This new operating system will teach you to transfer ownership of your daily burdens to God, and it is 100% sustainable.

Purchase your copy wherever books are sold

From
FELIX HALPERN

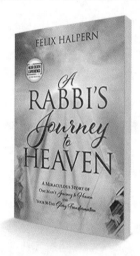

A Rabbi's Journey to Heaven

It all happened suddenly. In a twinkling of an eye. Rabbi Felix died, left his body, and crossed over into heaven. Amazed, he experienced the glories of heaven that he always read, pondered, and dreamt about. He also saw the lower realm, the second heaven, where demons dwell.

Three days after returning from heaven, God also gave Rabbi Felix a gift called "The Heavenly Soul Cleanse" which holds the keys to a transformational prayer life that turns our current prayer culture upside down. Rabbi Felix now lives from an open heaven, and as he shares these heavenly keys with you in this book, so will you. Imagine saturating your soul in heavenly glory and starving your soul from the natural order. As you do, God will heal your soul, and you will be launched into an entirely new operating system.

Take this journey with Rabbi Felix and experience this heavenly transformation. True freedom awaits you, and you will never be the same!

Purchase your copy wherever books are sold